UNLOCKING YOUR CHILD'S LEARNING POTENTIAL

HOW TO EQUIP KIDS TO SUCCEED IN SCHOOL & LIFE

CHERI FULLER

P.O. Box 35007, Colorado Springs, Colorado 80935

OUR GUARANTEE TO YOU

We believe so strongly in the message of our books that we are making this quality guarantee to you. If for any reason you are disappointed with the content of this book, return the title page to us with your name and address and we will refund to you the list price of the book. To help us serve you better, please briefly describe why you were disappointed. Mail your refund request to: PiñonPress, P.O. Box 35002, Colorado Springs, CO 80935.

Library of Congress Catalog Card Number:
94-17148
ISBN 08910-98348

Cover illustration: Anne Meskey

Some of the anecdotal illustrations in this book are true to life and are included with the permission of the persons involved. All other illustrations are composites of real situations, and any resemblance to people living or dead is coincidental.

Fuller, Cheri.
    Unlocking your child's learning potential : how to equip kids to succeed in school and life / Cheri Fuller.
        p. cm.
    Includes bibliographical references.
    ISBN 0-89109-834-8
    1. Learning ability. 2. Academic achievement. 3. Success.
LB1134.F85 1994
371.2'64—dc20   94-17148
                                                    CIP

Printed in the United States of America

6 7 8 9 10 11 12 13 14 15 / 05 04 03 02 01 00

Published in association with the literary agency of Alive Communications, P.O. Box 49068, Colorado Springs, CO 80949.

CONTENTS

To Holmes

ACKNOWLEDGMENTS

Special thanks to people who shared their experience, expertise, and encouragement with me: Karen DeClouet, Dr. Tim Campbell, Jerri Bell, Kaye Johns, Bitsy Thomas, Jane Henderson, Linda Swales, Jane Neidenfeuhr, Marilyn Morgan, Melanie Hemry, Lynn Fuller, Karen Gale, Kathy Veegeteveen, Bodie Thoene, Dr. John Sabolich, and many other parents and teachers who shared their insights about their own and their children's learning styles. Thank you to Donna Fullner for her computer help!

I am grateful to Liz Heaney, Traci Mullins, Kathy Yanni, and the Piñon Press staff, to Rick Christian and Michal Mardock of Alive Communications for believing that this book will be a valuable resource for parents.

Special love and thanks to my husband, Holmes, and our three wonderful children, Justin, Christopher, and Alison, for their willingness to help while I spent my days and nights at the computer, for their cheering me on, and their love. And to friends and family who cared and supported my work, thanks!

CHAPTER ONE

NO TWO CHILDREN LEARN ALIKE

C hildren want to be smart! In a recent survey, thousands of young people were asked the following: If you had a choice between being smart, having a lot of athletic ability, having a lot of money, or being beautiful—which would you choose? Forty-eight percent of the children said, "I want to be smart!" and valued school success and achievement—or as the researchers called it, "smartness"—above the other abilities or potentials. Twenty-five percent would rather have athletic ability. The highest priority for 20 percent of the children was more money. And only 7 percent chose beauty.

Unfortunately, although kids want to be smart, many are stymied in the classroom because they haven't learned to "study smart," they have different learning styles that are not addressed in the classroom, or they have learning problems. Millions of parents are bewildered and frustrated because the bright, curious, happy child they used to know has "shut down" to learning, is negative about school, and/or underachieves. Besides the over four million children labeled "learning disabled" who qualify for special resources, there are thousands of talented students who are doing just average or below average at school, and worse, are convinced they aren't very smart because of their lack of success in school.

As Mark Leibovich says, "Your early experiences at school can teach you—often for the first time—how you measure up. No matter how much you may accomplish later in life, a 'dumb' label stuck to you early on can leave a terrible scar."[1]

WHY ARE SOME CHILDREN NOT ACHIEVING?

Clint was a bright child who loved bike riding, baseball, and all other sports. Outgoing and well-liked at church and in the neighborhood, he was the best goalie on his soccer team. But although he tried hard, in the classroom he felt like a failure.

Clint came home in first and second grades feeling overwhelmed with the spelling words he had to learn. When he brought home papers he couldn't get done in class, or when ten-minute reading assignments took him an hour and a half, he broke down in tears. "This is too hard. I hate school," he cried day after day.

Although his mother did everything she could to help Clint, most homework sessions ended in frustration for Brenda, too. "It broke my heart to see Clint feel so badly about himself," she said. "There were many times I cried, wondering, 'Why is my child this way? Why is school so hard for him?'"

▽

Melissa's baby book had glowing reports of her verbal and social skills. "Melissa talked earlier than any of the other children—and hasn't stopped!" wrote her mother, Karen. She had a colorful vocabulary and could make conversation with anyone she met—and did at the grocery store, on their walks, or at the library. She had a bent for music and could remember jingles on television she'd heard only once or twice.

Melissa had some struggles in the early grades but learned to read, got reasonably good grades, always had a good relationship with her teachers, and liked school. When Melissa began lagging with her schoolwork in the fourth grade and, on many mornings, said, "I don't want to go to school," her mom grew worried. So Karen jumped in to help her with each homework assignment until it was complete, and told her how and when to get her work done. The trouble was, she became a taskmaster, and a power struggle between mother and daughter ensued.

Like most kids, Melissa tried hard to please her parents and teachers. She wanted to make good grades, but all she got were C's or lower. Already pigeonholed as slow in math and science, she spent part of her morning with the resource teacher and other "dumb kids" (as she called her group) who did extra work on basics. Although she was creative and could write a good story, her self-esteem plummeted.

Melissa's mom didn't realize her daughter was a learner who needed to hear and practice saying information, to be given clear explanations rather than being told to read directions in a book or on a work sheet. She had auditory and verbal strengths. But her teacher insisted that students be silent during study time and reread the textbook if they didn't understand, rather than explaining the difficult parts.

▽

Clint, like most hands-on learners, processed information best by being active while learning—by experiments, real-life projects, and manipulatives. But school was mostly letters and numbers, abstract symbols on work sheets or in textbooks that were hard to figure out. Often children have difficulties in school because their style of learning is different from the way the teacher teaches.

A recent Texas Education Agency survey found that 95 percent of secondary teachers in academic classes taught primarily with the lecture method.[2] But research tells us that only 25 percent of students have auditory strengths and benefit from a lecture method of instruction. While schools rely heavily on the textbook and lecture method, another 30 percent of students are visual learners who need to see slides, overhead projections, or pictures to learn. As many as 15 to 20 percent need "hands-on" experience, and 30 percent respond best to a mixture of several different teaching methods.[3]

Kids like Melissa and Clint have different learning styles, and unless someone intervenes, they wind up discouraged, in the low-track classes, and hating school. But there is a way they can be helped to overcome the obstacles, to learn and succeed—a way for them to develop and capitalize on their strengths and compensate for their weaknesses.

Let me say a word about teachers, because I'm not about to put them down. Teachers are some of my very favorite people—the teachers who inspired and taught me in school; my sister and sister-in-law, two of the best teachers I know; and friends who teach in schools across the country. I know how hard they work to make their courses interesting and how much they care about their students. Many teachers attend seminars and workshops to learn more about how to address the different learning styles of their students, but as a teacher myself I know how hard it is in a classroom—especially a large one— to teach in a way that reaches every single student.

After we attend a workshop on modalities, we often return to the classroom and teach right out of the learning/teaching style that is natural for us—because we concentrate most on content and getting assignments done and chapters covered. That's why I feel that, although discovering teaching strategies that meet the needs of students is helpful, learning-style information is *best* utilized by parents and students. This allows them to develop study strategies that work for their individual strengths, that help them overcome obstacles and adjust to any classroom situation—in short, that enable them to *learn how to learn any subject* and thus become active, motivated students.

HOW DO YOU LEARN?

Learning style entails how a person best takes in, understands, and remembers information. Psychologists have long known there are distinct personality types and that every person is different in many ways. Wouldn't it be boring if we were all the same? Those differences in preferences, choices of hobbies and clothing, and physical appearance such as red hair or blue or green eyes keep our families and world exciting and interesting.

Just as your child has a unique temperament and personality bent, he or she also has particular patterns and preferences for learning. According to experts at the National Learning Laboratory, the Center for the Study of Learning and Teaching Styles at Saint John's University, New York, and many other universities, many different factors make up a person's learning style and influence how we receive, store, and use information. Some of these factors are whether a child learns best independently, in a study group with peers, or in a highly structured classroom with an adult teaching. Some students need to see the big picture before breaking down a concept into parts, and some learn best in logical steps and want rules for doing new tasks. Some learn best in a quiet room, and others need some background noise.[4] This book covers different factors of learning styles: perceptual strengths, environmental factors, two different models of intelligence (Triarchic and Multiple Theory), right (global) and left-brained (analytic) thinking strategies.

As Dr. Priscilla Vail says, "Each person has patterns of strengths and weaknesses, clusters of likes and dislikes."[5] As you look at different factors in this book, you will find the *patterns* of your child's learning style—how not to label or pigeonhole your child as only one kind of learner, but to discover how your child learns best and how he or she can "study smarter."

Your child may be a verbalizer with auditory strengths who often repeats what the teacher said and needs to put the ideas into his or her own words. The child may have auditory strengths, linguistic and musical talent, an analytical thinking approach that requires things to be presented "in order," or he may learn best in a group. She may be an early-morning learner who needs a little background music to concentrate and does best on a test or assignment when she has bright light. Or your child may be a hands-on, exploratory type of learner who remembers best through concrete experiences and loves activities in which he has materials to manipulate and demonstrate concepts.

What's important is that research has shown that students achieve more when they learn in environments best suited to their personal learning styles, when new or difficult information is introduced through their strongest modalities, and when they know how to capitalize on their strengths in their study time.[6]

And we know that school problems arise when the child learns visually (or another way) and the teacher teaches in a strongly auditory way, and at the same time doesn't recognize or build on the child's strength. Frustration builds and learning can be blocked.

PERCEPTUAL STRENGTHS

Of all the factors of learning style, one that plays a vital role in studying, understanding, and remembering information—the one factor that has the greatest impact upon how your child learns—is *perceptual strength*. That's a fancy way of indicating the sense through which children take in information:

- Whether they learn best by seeing (reading, observing, looking at pictures and diagrams)—that is, by *visual learning*.
- Whether they learn best by hearing explanations and talking about the information—that is, by *auditory learning*.
- Whether they need to get their muscles, movement, and/or touch involved in learning (by doing an experiment, rehearsing, or taking an active approach)—that is, by *kinesthetic learning*.
- Whether they need to combine methods to understand and learn.

While most of us learn in all three ways, scientists have discovered that in most children one sense is usually more finely tuned and influential for learning than the others.

We can compare the learner to a television set that can receive information on several different channels. Unless you have cable television, one channel usually comes in more clearly than the others. And just as you would tend to watch that stronger, clearer channel as the main source of your news and entertainment, the learner tends to rely on one means—the auditory, visual, or kinesthetic—as the primary way of receiving and processing information, and of expressing knowledge and ideas.[7]

If one station has constant interference and is blocked from effective use and the student doesn't know how to change channels, he can become frustrated and develop problems in the classroom.

Helen Keller's visual and auditory channels were not available for processing information or learning words. But when her sense of touch—her strength—was tapped into to get through to her brain, the light bulb went on and she understood language. If we discover children's strengths, their mental growth can be enhanced and they can be more successful in school and life.

Let me give you an example. When our son Justin was in the tenth grade, he was assigned to memorize a long British poem from the 1800s for English class. No one, the teacher said, would receive a passing grade for the course without reciting the eight-stanza poem in its entirety in front of the class.

Justin silently read over the poem several times each night and when his turn came, got up to recite the poem. However, he could remember only three stanzas, not nearly enough to pass. In frustration, he worked on the poem several more days and then tried again. This time he got through five stanzas. He would have one more chance, the teacher informed him, to recite the whole poem.

That day after school I gave him a blank tape and suggested that he read the whole poem on tape, listen to it, and recite along with it while driving to and from school, sports, and his part-time job. I knew Justin's strengths were in listening and talking and that he needed to both hear and say the information to master it. And he was just desperate enough at that point to try my suggestion!

After applying this strategy for a few days, Justin was able to get up in class and recite the poem from beginning to end, word perfect. By tapping into his learning strengths, he succeeded in an otherwise frustrating and difficult assignment.

Discovering children's learning styles *is* a key to success and achievement in school. It gives hope to kids who have never known any success in school and helps bright children become more aware of their talents. It's not a program, but a way of seeing patterns of strengths and developing a different perspective on your child's learning. It's not a panacea for all learning problems, but even students who have been labeled "learning disabled" *can* compensate for their weaknesses and achieve more when we discover and use their skills and talents.

Sometimes educational and/or diagnostic testing is needed to determine the causes and range of a child's school-related problems. School psychometricians can assess a child's abilities, and the local university's learning centers and education professors or developmental specialists are excellent sources of diagnostic testing and professional evaluation.

ONE TEACHER'S EXPERIENCE WITH LEARNING STYLES

Julie, a teacher in California, had a very personal experience with learning styles. She had been a successful, mostly A college student when she suffered a cerebral hemorrhage that resulted in paralysis on her right side. Before this, her academic strengths were visual and kinesthetic. She read a great deal, but when studying for a test, she wrote items to be learned over and over again until they were memorized. Just reading didn't seem to be enough. Writing was an essential ingredient.

After her hemorrhage, her study habits had to change. "I could no longer even write lecture notes in class, never mind use writing as a study tool," says Julie. She had to learn by careful listening. To study, she had her friends ask her questions. If she did not have the answer, they provided an oral one, she repeated it, and went on to the next question. Later, she discovered that she could eliminate the need for another person by using a tape recorder. She taped professors' lectures and played the tapes to rehearse and study in her car and in her dorm room.

Julie's experience shows that we can use different modalities and develop other strategies to study, and even with great obstacles, be successful. But she had never capitalized on her experience in her teaching until she attended my summer seminar on learning styles and motivating kids.

"When school started," says Julie, "I was eager to start the year out right. I had the class make flash cards together for the first history test. I guided them all the way. Then I used these flash cards to make an audiotape. I asked a question, waited five or more seconds, and gave the answer. I made copies for all students I have evaluated to have auditory strengths."

She also used the tape for a spelling-bee game in which the students line up. If a student can answer a question before the tape does, he or she goes to the end of the line. If the student cannot, he or she sits down. Julie also created some fast-paced team games using the tape recorder. Then after convincing the students and parents of the value of these tapes, she offered an after-school audiotape workshop in which she showed students how to make their own study tapes. The student goes through a current batch of study cards, recording each question, waiting five or more seconds, and then giving the answer.

As students' grades came up and some of the most frustrated kids got excited about learning, Julie also began to receive positive feedback from parents. "I can't believe what you have done for my daughter," said one mother of a formerly low-achieving child. "She came home with her study cards, made her own tape, studied it by herself, and got an A on the history test. Before, I would have had to spend hours helping her, pushing her, and not have the same wonderful result. With her own tape, she can listen to it at home, or in the car to and from school, and show off for her brothers and sisters (who also learn the answer). The sessions are short and rather painless."

"You are the first teacher in five years to try to find out what learning style is best for my daughter," said another mother. "We've been very frustrated in the past. Now that she has some active ways to study, and I know how to help her at home, she's more confident and making better grades."

SUCCEEDING IN SCHOOL

Just as Julie found in her classroom, teaching our children *how* to learn is as important as teaching them *what* to learn, because research shows that kids who are taught and study in ways that match their learning preferences—whether auditory, visual, kinesthetic, or a combination of methods—have the following advantages:

- They concentrate better, retain more, and make higher grades. In 1986, Maurine Martini won a national award for her research with high school science students. She read a chapter from a science textbook onto tape and entered one chapter into a computer. She found auditory learners achieved higher scores with the tape and printed book. Visual students did better reading from the book than listening. And kinesthetic/tactile learners did best with the material on computer. All students, however, improved scores when the computer was added.[8]
- They acquire a positive view of learning. Children's early learning experience, whether a string of successes or failures, strongly influences their motivation and view of themselves as learners. If they use their strengths and are successful in learning to read and in all the early experiences of elementary school, they have a solid foundation to build on.
- They become more active, independent learners. They "learn how to learn" and maximize the study time they have at home or school.
- They can learn to adapt to different teaching styles in the classroom.
- When they hit a snag, or are "stuck" in a subject or task that is difficult, they have tools—just as you have jumper cables in your car for when your battery runs down, or a spare tire for blowouts—to draw on, get over the obstacles, and learn what they need to.
- Homework conflict between parents and children can be eliminated, resulting in more family harmony.

You see, children in the same family rarely learn the same way; husbands and wives usually have distinct learning styles, and parents often approach tasks in different ways from their children. (In a later chapter we will look at your learning style as a parent.) This can be a real problem! The parent whose main learning mode is auditory may interpret a kinesthetic style as misbehavior. The visual parent may say "Be quiet!" to her auditory learner, who needs to say and hear the information to understand and remember it, thus blocking the child's best means of study.

For example, Jamie was a fifth grader who was burned out on schoolwork and considered by his teachers and parents to be an underachiever. His dad, a very visual, reflective (and quiet!) accountant, expected Jamie to sit still when he studied and exerted pressure and even grounded him when his grades were not high enough or when he "played around" during homework times.

However, for kinesthetic learners, "being still" requires so much mental energy that they can't concentrate on their work. Jamie was a "doer" who needed an active approach to studying. Evening homework times became a war zone.

When Jamie had a lot of facts to learn for the Geography Bowl, I suggested his mom let him use his muscles in the practice sessions. While Meredith fired off the questions from the couch, Jamie bounced his Nerf basketball and shot a basket with each answer. "Something happened while he was active," his mom said. "He got a better imprint somehow on his memory. It also helped his focus and concentration." After their daily basketball/geography sessions, Jamie won the right to represent his grade in the schoolwide Geography Bowl. And although he was the youngest student in the finals, competing against even eighth graders, he placed third—his first scholastic recognition ever. Using this approach and a white chalkless board to practice vocabulary and spelling words, and some other study strategies that used his strengths, he became one of the top students in his grade.

In addition to developing a more positive attitude toward his homework and himself as a learner, Jamie felt more affirmed by his dad. Some of the stress was removed from their relationship. Pleased with Jamie's achievement, Dad spent less time criticizing and more time supporting his active, hands-on approach to learning.

As Dr. James Dobson, Focus on the Family president and an

auditory learner who said he couldn't have achieved as much in graduate school in psychology without his tape recorder and tapes to study with, observed that one of the best ways to instill self-confidence is to teach methods by which the child can *compensate*. Compensation "means the individual counterbalances his weaknesses by capitalizing on his strengths. It is our job as parents to help our children find those strengths and learn to exploit them for all the self-satisfaction they will yield." That's what this book will help you to do.

AS INDIVIDUAL AS FINGERPRINTS

While I will describe characteristics of learners who show auditory, kinesthetic, or visual strengths, keep in mind that each child's brain is just as unique and individual as his or her fingerprint. No two students think and process information exactly alike. Although we know boys' and girls' brains develop differently and that people with a visual bent share some characteristics, there are also differences in talents, gifts, and ways they approach a task. And while most people have a strongest modality, about 30 percent have what we call "mixed modalities," or two perceptual strengths they use interchangeably. So as you read the characteristics and descriptions of the different learning styles, remember not to pigeonhole your child but keep in mind that he or she has a distinct pattern of strengths and weaknesses and is developing new abilities and skills continually as he or she grows up.

LEARNING DIFFERENCES OR LEARNING DISABILITIES?

The word *disability* literally means "incapable": the inability to pursue an occupation or task because of physical or mental impairment. Educators are beginning to acknowledge that much of what is termed "learning disabilities" is really a matter of unique learning differences and variations in learning styles. The whole topic of learning disabilities is complex and controversial. Not even special education experts agree on exactly what a learning disability is.

As Dr. Lauren Bradway says, "Partly because there is no universally accepted test battery to confirm such a condition's existence, the definition of 'learning disability' can differ not only from state to state, but even between neighboring school systems."[9] Some school districts, she says, consider a thirty-point discrepancy between a child's scores on the visual-motor and language segments of an IQ test to be an indication of learning disability. Others say that even a ten-point difference reveals a learning disability.[10]

Learning-different, variations in learning, or even academically challenged are better terms than disabled or "not able to learn." Some of these kids may not be able to learn as quickly in one situation but learn very effectively in another. Sometimes the student is missing a step in the learning process or needs help connecting the sound of the word, the concept, with the picture in his mind.[11] Psychometrists (who do educational testing, write evaluations and individual education plans, and measure psychological variables) report that some children referred to as "learning disabled" are kinesthetic learners who have not been shown how to use their strengths and develop other learning channels. When the teacher uses only visual and auditory methods, the kinesthetic learners in the class often exhibit behavior problems.

However, when we pin negative labels on children they begin to believe them. Their expectations for themselves are lowered, and they develop a passivity psychologists call "learned helplessness," and give up trying. Many times as a teacher I was saddened to hear students reply to an assignment for the whole class, "I can't read that book or write that essay; I'm LD."

I agree with experts like Dr. Priscilla Vail who says that "the term 'learning disability' has an air of finality that promotes pessimistic thinking at home and at school."[12] That's why in this book I refer to learning styles and differences, strengths and weaknesses (which we all have), instead of disabilities. When students are taught strategies to manage weaknesses and capitalize on their strengths and when modifications are made in the classroom, there is hope and progress.

Instead of a label, children with learning differences or challenges need to have supportive parents and teachers who know they are not lazy or stupid and instead look for their gifts and strengths and have high expectations for them. They often need someone to tutor or help them in certain parts of their learning process and/or in certain subjects. They need to know they may have to work harder than some classmates (but in the process, they'll learn perseverance and character qualities that will be valuable for a lifetime). They need positive role models and people to mentor them in their fields of talent and interest. They need someone to be their advocate with the schools and help them overcome failure and setbacks, while encouraging dreams and goals and providing the support to achieve them.

A child with problems at school or trouble with learning certain subjects or skills may need careful evaluation to see whether there is a problem with vision or hearing, neurological damage, speech, dyslexia, or attention deficit. A child with severe learning problems needs all the help that school, home, and community resources can give. Sometimes there is a developmental delay, and the child is a "late bloomer." Remember, many slow-maturing children are extremely bright and can achieve great things with parents' and teachers' patience, help, and encouragement.

TAKING ACTION

Instead of expecting your child to learn just like you do, talk to your child about his or her learning preferences. If your child could choose to practice math facts or vocabulary words in any way possible, how would he or she do it? Read the chapter about parents' learning style to get a better picture of how you prefer to learn. Read the descriptions of children and take the surveys for your child in chapter 3. After talking about how your child learns best and what his or her strengths are, encourage your child to study that way, no matter how different it seems.

Next, try some of the study strategies suggested throughout the pages that follow and see which methods—or combinations of methods—help your child learn and remember important information. Teach your child how to take a lesson or textbook material and change it into materials he or she can learn from—whether it be a game, audiotape, mind map, computer, time line on the bedroom wall, or study cards.

Be sure to take "Another Look at Smart" in chapters 9 and 10 to discover your child's special gifts and talents. Every child has at least one intelligence gift, or more likely, a combination of talents related to his or her learning style. Not just 5 percent of students are "gifted," as standardized IQ testing might lead you to believe. Exciting research on intelligence shows there are many combinations of abilities that make up talent. We'll look at ways to identify and develop the different gifts your child has.

As you gain insights and find study methods that work for your child, share your understanding about learning style with the teacher and ask what he or she has observed in class about how your child learns. (Chapter 11 will give you suggestions on working with teachers without alienating them.) When teachers are aware of learning style in the classroom, and when parents understand their children's strengths and show them how to capitalize on them, kids can excel. D and F failures can be turned into A and B successes, confidence grows, and children become active learners with a pattern of achievement at school.

CHAPTER TWO

LEARNING-DIFFERENT PEOPLE WHO ACHIEVED

When John was in grade school, the teachers wanted to flunk him out of every grade. His mother would go up to school and plead with them, assuring them she would work with him at home. John became more and more afraid of learning. "I remember in fourth, fifth, and sixth grades, I'd hide in the bathroom so the teachers wouldn't see me during tests. I avoided everything I could," said John. He felt like a dunce in the classroom and a reject on the playground—he was last to be chosen for teams at recess or PE class. Reading was a struggle for John. He could figure out a few words, but not well enough or fast enough to pass.

Instead, John would draw pictures of rocket ships, flying saucers, and planes, or he'd invent little steam engines and spacecraft. His hero was Leonardo da Vinci. While everyone was taking a test, he was daydreaming and doodling on paper how the latest rocket or airplane could work. After school he mixed up rocket fuel and tried to build the machines he designed and get them to fly. "I also went to my dad's prosthetics office (where artificial limbs are made and fitted for amputees), and it was fun to watch him help kids walk again. I was intrigued by his tools. The work seemed creative and interesting, and there was no written work to do! I decided I wanted to help amputees walk and have normal lives like my dad did."[1]

In seventh grade, John brought his report card home with seven F's. Prior to seventh grade the students were graded with checks and minuses, so his dad didn't really know how bad his grades were. "Dad came unglued that night; he ranted and railed and said I wasn't going to amount to anything." John still remembers that night, crying about his failure until sunrise. "It was very traumatic. I decided that night that no matter what, I would show everybody in the world that I can do it.

"I envisioned myself in a race car at the back of the pack, and I had to catch up and win." John started staying up until 2:00 a.m. to get homework done. It took him a long time to do everything, but he was determined to catch up. He got a tutor to help him learn and pass the next courses. A very patient and knowledgeable retired teacher, she helped him in reading and math and other subjects.

After constant work, John brought his grades up to C's, then to B's the next year. Then finally in late high school he got straight A's. It took tremendous effort, and the work and late hours made him more and more nervous, which has caused him some lifetime problems with stress. He began working for his father at age thirteen, and by sixteen he decided to follow in his father's footsteps.

By graduation, John's goal was to study prosthetics and orthotics at New York University; he was first in his class and interned for a year. From his hard work in high school, he had taught himself the most efficient ways to study: underlining and highlighting important areas, learning how to skim pages for main ideas, and learning how to take quick notes and zero in on what the professor was saying or get notes from someone else. A visual/spatial learner, John was strong in remembering diagrams and pictures, not words. "If you drew me a picture I could understand it, but just words left me cold," said John. Realizing his strengths, he was able to increase his ability to learn abstractly. He also has incredible dexterity in his hands, as well as creative problem-solving, engineering, and design skill.

"Everything was late for me; I got better at sports, but not until much later in high school," he said. As his kinesthetic abilities increased, so did his visual and spatial talent. As was true in his school years, the auditory style is not his preference or strength. He still finds listening to seminars boring unless there are slides, videos, or a chalktalk—or if he's extremely interested in the subject.

John Sabolich, who almost flunked out of elementary school, is now the world's most famous inventor of specialized, high-tech prostheses out of lightweight composites. His inventions include the "Oklahoma City Running Leg"; the "Sabolich Foot," a foot made of elastic futuristic materials that absorb vertical shock and convert it to energy; and a bionic myoelectric arm that doctors call a technological wonder.

Because of his determination, innovation, and technical ability, amputees all over the world are jumping for joy, dancing, cheerleading, running in races, skydiving, and living normal lives again. The Sabolich Prosthetic and Research Center in Oklahoma City has even designed a sense-of-feel system to provide patients "feeling" in their artificial feet. Sabolich authored a book entitled *You're Not Alone*, the personal stories of thirty-eight amputees who faced the physical challenges of amputation and found the courage to go on with their lives.

LEARNING DIFFERENCES AND GIFTS

Is Sabolich's strong three-dimensional thinking ability and visual-spatial style of learning a disability or a difference? Is a fox disabled because his hearing is so sharp he can hear a sound twenty miles away and yet can't fly? By having a weakness in one area, another sense or ability is heightened. I believe it is a learning difference *and a gift* that has enabled Sabolich to help thousands of people with physical handicaps and disabilities. Like Sabolich, there are many famous people who have had learning differences that caused them problems or struggles in school, and yet out of these very differences emerged the talents, skills, and intelligence that enabled them to make a great impact on their community and world.

Winston Churchill had problems in reading, suffered from a speech defect, and was hyperactive. He was placed in the lowest form (grade), where the slow boys were taught English.[2] Albert Einstein failed several math courses in his school career. His teachers said he was too much of a daydreamer and too slow. Louis Pasteur failed the entrance exams to medical school and was known as a hardworking plodder. Thomas Edison had severe memory problems and said of school, "I remember that I was never able to get along at school. I was always at the foot of the class. I used to feel that the teachers did not sympathize with me, and that my father thought I was stupid."[3] Author and poet Amy Lowell had math problems, and Woodrow Wilson, who did not learn the letters of the alphabet until he was nine, became the twenty-seventh president of the United States.[4]

Whether they had terrible handwriting, trouble with spelling, or difficulty with abstract math concepts or reading, they found ways to bypass or compensate for their weaknesses. What mattered most for each of them was focusing and capitalizing on their strengths, developing a vision and hope for the future, and applying the determination and perseverance to do what it took to reach their goals. Not all of the people in my learning-different hall of fame have become world famous, but all have made significant contributions.

Fred Epstein was not a good student in his early school years. His grades in college were only average, and in chemistry they were terrible. Yet he was determined to become a doctor. After being turned down by four medical schools, he gained admittance to New York Medical College (thanks to his psychiatrist father's intervention) and became a pediatric neurosurgeon who has made a career of doing what medicine said could not be done: operating on and removing lethal tumors from the tiny brain stems of children.[5]

Epstein takes on cases that other neurosurgeons won't touch. His willingness to take calculated risks, his fierce determination, his incredible technical skill, and his refusal to accept defeat has enabled him to move neurosurgery to frontiers thought impossible a decade ago and in the process save the lives of countless children.[6]

Another student, whose weakness in the auditory modality made first grade a nightmare, turned her school problems into help and hope for many school-age children and their counselors.

"I ran away from first grade six times!" said Jane Henderson, a school counselor in Texas whose visual and kinesthetic skills propelled her to develop a counseling program on computer to help troubled kids express and deal with their feelings. "The first grade teacher yelled at me during oral drill because I could not count to one hundred." Since first grade was a lot of auditory work, oral repetition of phonics rules and sounds, and oral instruction, and her strengths were visual and kinesthetic, she was miserable in school.

"In fact," said Jane, "I finally learned to read before the fourth grade from an aunt who was a third-grade teacher." Every day in the summer Jane walked to her aunt's house for instruction. Not only was her aunt very caring and patient, she also boosted Jane's self-esteem and, realizing her learning style was visual and kinesthetic (long before the learning-style approach was written up in educational journals), used visual cues and creative, active ways of teaching her to read.

Jane was a fairly good student in high school but still had some struggles. Her ninth-grade algebra teacher was rigid and highly auditory. She sat the students with 100 percent in the front seats, and the others in order of their grade rank in the class. The results were abysmal: Jane failed the course and had to repeat it in summer school. The next time she took algebra the course was taught by a teacher who did a lot of hands-on learning and had students working problems at the board (kinesthetic and visual). Jane completed the course with a 98-percent average. "Every time someone attacked me, I failed; but if they built me up, I succeeded," Jane said.

Jane uses her skills to build up many students, and she has a special compassion for anyone who struggles to learn. She also developed abilities in music, public speaking, and computers. She has a gift for humor, has written a book, and teaches a seminar to help other counselors and teachers who work with children, entitled "Counseling with Computers: Technology and Techniques." Jane has high expectations for kids and shows them ways to use their strengths to study and achieve the very best.

"I was only eight years old," wrote Bodie Thoene, an award-winning author, in her book *Writer to Writer*, "but already I was a failure.

In most of those things that measure success for a third grader, I had failed." As she tried to figure out how she could break the news to her parents, she stared at her report card.

"Math: C . . . not so bad. Spelling: F . . . disaster. Reading: F . . . major disaster. Conduct: C . . . oh, well. Effort: E . . . my life was over," Bodie said. The teacher had called her lazy. One of the boys had called her stupid. "Could I be both of those terrible things? It was the blackest day of my eight-year-old life, for I knew I had disappointed my parents. Mama called me bright. Daddy called me his little 'go-getter.' Didn't this report card repudiate everything they believed about me?"[7]

Fortunately for Bodie, her parents continued to believe in her. That summer, they found an enthusiastic tutor who helped her learn to read and to express her own thoughts on paper. From third grade on, her dream was to be a writer. School continued to be a struggle. High school was the most difficult and traumatic experience of her life, except for a teacher who encouraged her creative writing. In spite of her D's in English (because of mechanics), Mrs. Gaede saw Bodie's incredible grasp of language. Math was like a foreign language, and it nearly kept her from graduating from high school. She had spelling problems and trouble in reading. She learned foreign languages quickly if taught in a conversational approach, but the grammar was difficult.

Bodie compensated with her sharp auditory skills. And her ability to hear dialogue and write the way real people think and talk enabled her to be a successful scriptwriter for John Wayne movies. A picture-visual learner, Bodie told such convincing tall tales as a child that people believed them to be true. Her great imagination enables her to "see" in her mind's eye the scenes in the historical fiction she and her husband, Brock, write. Five of their novels have won awards. Brock does the research and compiles the facts, and Bodie makes it entertainment.

Another nominee for learning-different honors is Greg Louganis, Olympic gold medalist. When Greg started school, he was laughed at and made fun of because of his shyness and his speech and reading difficulties. His serious school problems and failures produced much frustration. "I decided to direct all my time and energy into something I could be proficient in," said Louganis. He wanted to show people he could do something, and because he both enjoyed and was skilled at dancing, tumbling, gymnastics, and diving, he honed his kinesthetic talents. Dr. Sammy Lee, a former Olympic diving champion, spotted the troubled thirteen-year-old at a competition, took him under his wing, and began to coach him. With a constant need to improve, Louganis began to excel in diving; made the U.S. Olympic team at sixteen; earned a drama degree at University of California, Irvine; and by age twenty-eight had won forty-seven national titles, six world championships, three Olympic medals, three world cups, and many other awards.[8]

With the rhythm and grace of a dancer, the strength and power of a weight lifter, and the agility and perfect timing of a gymnast, Louganis continued to set world records. When he was honored with the Jesse Owens Foundation award as the finest athlete in the world in 1987, he said in his acceptance message, "Who would believe that an adopted kid of Samoan heritage, who was laughed at in school because he talked funny, would one day be spoken of in the same breath as Jesse Owens and all the other magnificent athletes who have been honored by winning this award?"[9]

WHAT CAN WE LEARN?

What can we learn from the stories of these people? What can we apply to motivate and encourage our children to be the best they can be? In all these people, their drive and determination go back to their difficult times as children. Although they had big obstacles to overcome, those very obstacles were what propelled them to set goals, find strategies to overcome the barriers, and achieve. Each had weaknesses, but each had corresponding strengths and gifts as well.

In each learning-different person who made it there was another striking similarity: someone came alongside to give assistance, tutoring, and encouragement, and to see the "positives" instead of focusing on the negatives or the failures. For Bodie Thoene it was her parents and the teacher who tutored her in reading all summer, who realized Bodie couldn't learn with phonics and used another method to teach her. For John Sabolich it was a tutor who helped him get caught up and learn how to study, and a dad who allowed him to work at his clinic as a teenager. For Greg Louganis it was a man who saw his potential as an Olympic diver years before he won, and volunteered to coach him.

Whether it was a parent, relative, teacher, or tutor who acted as mentor, they made all the difference. If you have a learning-different child, consider his or her gifts and strengths, and with the information in this book set about to discover and capitalize on them! Here are some ways to make a world of difference in a child's life.

Whatever the Child's Strengths

Focus on the positives rather than the negatives. Whether your child likes to paint abstract watercolors, tinker with computers, play the drums, write stories, or fix lawnmowers, accept and highlight those unique strengths, even if they are not your cup of tea! We may not prize a certain skill or possess it ourselves, but if we nurture the seed of a talent in our child today, in years to come and with practice and hard work, it may develop into a fulfilling hobby or even career. Don't equate success with only school-related/academic pursuits. For some young people, "especially bodily-kinesthetic or spatial learners, blooming in life may have more to do with achieving success in artistic, mechanical, or athletic areas."[10] In chapters 9 and 10, "Another Look at Smart," I will give characteristics of different kinds of intelligence and giftedness.

Respect individuality in your family. Your child may not have the sports ability of the rest of your family, but prefers art or music. Or he or she may not have the "math smarts" his or her siblings do but is mechanically talented. When uniqueness is respected in a family, it frees each child or teen to develop his or her own personality and special talents.

Be aware that as your child grows, new skills and talents will develop. Although Tom Lough showed logical-math and musical talent in his school years, his kinesthetic and thus athletic abilities bloomed late. At age twenty-five he made the U.S. Olympic team in the modern pentathlon. And his interpersonal, or people, skills have continued to develop into his forties.

Show your child you value his or her work, even early attempts. Have a special frame to hang the newest painting. Perhaps you could save a wall in the house for a gallery of framed drawings and paintings. Send off your budding writer's best poems to a children's magazine, and enter science projects in school science fairs and young inventors' exhibits and contests. Encourage entrepreneurial efforts if your child shows business savvy and wants to try out ideas for making money.

Don't criticize or squelch your child's enthusiasm. Refrain from comments like, "You aren't playing that piece on the piano again!" or "What's *that?*" when looking at your child's abstract watercolor painting. Rather, support your child's endeavors. Your words of encouragement are powerful motivators for your child's developing talent!

Luciano Pavarotti, the great opera singer, tells about his father's and grandmother's encouragement and what it meant to him. As a young boy, his grandmother put him on her lap while he enthusiastically hummed an Italiam nursery rhyme and said, "You're going to be great, you'll see." He was a poor student in school but was excellent in communicating with people. His mother dreamed he'd be a successful banker. Instead, he taught elementary school and sang infrequently. "But my father constantly goaded me, saying I was singing below my potential," Pavarotti said. Finally, at age twenty-two, he quit teaching and started selling insurance to provide time and money to develop his vocal talent. He says studying voice with an outstanding teacher was the turning point of his life. "It's a mistake to take the safe path in life. If I hadn't listened to my father and dropped teaching, I would never be here. And yes, my teacher groomed me. But no teacher ever told me I would become famous. Just my grandmother."[11]

Help your child learn to deal with failure and bounce back without being devastated. When an experiment or project doesn't work, say, "It's okay, because scientists fail their way to success."

You can point out that Jonas Salk failed countless times before finding a polio vaccine that stopped a worldwide epidemic, and that Edison failed hundreds of times before he developed the light bulb. Whether it's a musical tryout your child failed, a team he didn't make, or a science fair she didn't win, let him know you love him dearly regardless of his performance, and that he is a special, important part of your family. Help him or her look at the failures or setbacks and say, "What can I learn from this?" and go on. Be prepared to accept incomplete projects and even a change of direction as your child finds what to try next time.

Talk to the teacher about your child's strengths and how these could be maximized at school. Kathy, a Michigan mom, shared with her son David's teacher at the first of the year that he loved to work and carry responsibility. So she gave David the job of being Computer Lab monitor. Every morning he came early to uncover and turn on the computers. Each afternoon following classes he stayed and cleaned up the lab, turned off and covered all the computers. David never missed a day the entire year and was so responsible they put two students under his supervision in the computer lab. He had some other academic challenges he was working on in the classroom, but recognizing and developing one of his strengths at school built his confidence and self-esteem.

Provide a support system. All of us have weaknesses and need support of some kind—a calculator to speed up math computation, a tutor to teach some new study strategies, glasses or contacts to improve weak vision, or a computer with spell-check capacity to facilitate composing written essays and reports. Stephen Cannell is a successful, creative television writer and producer who has produced over two dozen prime-time series. His talent is writing, but his weakness in reading causes him to transpose numbers and letters and to have trouble with spelling and sequencing. Instead of spending his time trying to correct the problems that have plagued him since childhood, he dictates scripts for his assistant or types them on computer and has an assistant proofread and polish the rough places.[12]

Find out what help your child needs and *provide that support!*

The chapters that follow and chapter 11, "Your Child in the Class-room," will provide many ways to compensate for weaknesses, build on strengths, and meet needs without letting negative labels attach themselves to your child.

CHAPTER THREE

IDENTIFYING YOUR CHILD'S LEARNING STYLE

D id you know that the word *teacher* or *educator* means "one who brings out the best in the student"? As parents, we are our children's first and best teachers. The more you know your child, the more you can help your child have successful learning experiences and develop and use his or her strengths—and encourage his or her teachers to do the same. As a parent, you are actually better equipped than a teacher—with twenty or thirty students in a classroom—to discover this valuable information about your child, to notice how the child tackles a problem and what method of study he or she turns to when under stress or time pressure.

Your child's learning style is as individual as his or her fingerprint and reflects his or her development, aptitudes, strengths, and weaknesses. Remember that there is no right or wrong learning style. That is just another way that people are different. Let's look at three basic areas of strength that will help you as a parent identify and understand how your child learns best.

CLUES TO LEARNING STRENGTHS

Think back to the last time you took your child to a mall. Did your child wander off gazing at things that caught his or her eye? If you panicked because you couldn't find your child, did you discover him or her looking at the merchandise in a different aisle? As a grown-up, this visually oriented person can go to the grocery store for several items, get sidetracked looking at things, and come home an hour and a half later. My husband's mom, Joan, said that Holmes' wandering off to look at things was a frequent occurrence in his childhood. During more than one outing to the park, she found him in the top of a big tree looking around (up there he had a better view). They lost him in Cave of the Winds and found him gazing intently at stalactites on the roof and sides of the cavern. At a large, old historic hotel where they stopped to eat and tour, he knew the whole hotel and all the corridors and back entrances within an hour from his investigating and observing.

Perhaps your child wanders off to touch and feel the merchandise—much to the saleslady's and your dismay—and likes to twirl the racks around and around (getting lost inside the clothes), and open doors and climb on anything available in the dressing room. In a toy store these "doers," or kinesthetic children, have to be closely supervised because if left to their own devices, they may take apart a game or toy to see how it works.

If your verbal, auditory child gets lost, you may find him or her talking to another child, making friends with a saleslady, or talking someone out of a quarter for a big jawbreaker from the machine. Not liking to be alone, your child will look for someone to play with or chat with.

READING PREFERENCES

Look at your child's reading preferences. Auditory/verbal learners enjoy stories with dialogue and good characters. They respond well to phonics reading programs. They love to listen to a good story, but also enjoy role-playing and acting it out. Discussing the story and their feelings about it and talking about alternative endings, also heighten their interest.

Kinesthetic, hands-on learners like action stories and science fiction, and adventure tales best of all. They need to read in short segments with breaks rather than in long sittings, and if someone doesn't help them find books in their particular interest areas, they may not like reading at all. They'd rather be active or playing outside.

A kinesthetic learner I had in English class rarely reads a novel (in fact, I don't know if he finished a single novel during his high school career), but he will read a 250-page motorcycle manual over a weekend, because of his intense interest in the subject. For kinesthetic learners to be successful in reading, it is very important that a multisensory reading program be used in the early stages of learning to read.

Visual learners tend to like reading but thoroughly enjoy pictures and photos in books. Sight vocabulary and context clues should be emphasized in building their reading skills. (More about reading and analysis of reading programs that best suit the different learning styles in chapter 8, "How Learning Styles Impact Reading Skills.") Visual learners who aren't engulfed in too much television watching or video-game playing can actually become the children most "hooked on books."

To determine the learning style in a very young child, you may want to read aloud a story to him or her that has a refrain of some sort, like "and the rabbit went hop, hop, hop" or "there once was a boy with a little toy drum; with a rat-a-tat-tat and a rum-y-tum-tum." When you read the refrain, does your child

- Get up close (maybe insisting on sitting on your lap) to see the pictures? This indicates visual strengths.
- Mimic the words of the refrain or interrupt to talk about the story? This indicates auditory strengths.
- Move around and do what the refrain says—hop, jump, or whatever action the book suggests? This indicates kinesthetic strengths.

LEARNING STYLES IN PROGRESS

As Donna, a mother of three, said, "I watch my just-turned three-year-old and know he will be a strong auditory learner. From a young age, he was proficient with his descriptions of events and objects. And although he is the youngest, he is the first one to respond to my verbal requests." When observed carefully, even infants show a bent or preference for one style or another. My visual baby Chris could be entertained by watching his colorful mobile or a bird outside the window. My most auditory son, Justin, was an early talker and responded best to my voice or music if he was upset.

Yet as babies grow mentally, physically, and emotionally, their learning styles are also developing. From infancy to kindergarten and first grade, children tend to learn kinesthetically or with a hands-on approach—by touching, feeling, crawling, and emptying out your kitchen drawer. That's why the most successful preschool program, developed by Maria Montessori, built on children's natural strengths with manipulatives, concrete materials, and direct experience.

By first or second grade, children's visual skills are developing, which is why reading instruction is begun at that age. The visual skills are not totally developed until fourth grade. And some children are what we call "late bloomers"—their visual skills may be delayed, which could cause difficulty in learning to read.

By fifth or sixth grade (and later for some children), the auditory or listening skills are stronger. That's why a teacher of sixth graders might give a thirty-minute presentation on the causes of the Civil War and expect the students to take notes, whereas if a kindergarten teacher did that, we'd wonder about her teaching skills and understanding of children. But just because some children may be delayed in developing kinesthetically, auditorially, or visually, that doesn't mean they won't develop those skills!

"Children's brains start out immature," says Dr. Larry Silver, clinical professor of psychiatry at the Georgetown University School of Medicine. "Maturational spurts occur once or twice a year. It's as if a new computer chip enters in. And when that chip starts firing, there may be changes in the way a child learns."[1] Children are always learning, always developing. And that's good news!

Visual Learning: Luke

Luke, a child with visual strengths, is a perceptive "watcher" who processes and remembers information best by picturing something in his mind's eye and maintaining a mental image of it. This child has such a good visual memory, it's like he has a copy machine in his head. His mental Xeroxer will come in handy later in the classroom for spelling tests, reading comprehension, and studying for tests.

As a little child, though, Luke was described by his mother as "placid"—his calmness and tendency to entertain himself were often due to his fascination and interest in his visual surroundings. He could be quieted by just seeing Mom or Dad's face appear at his door or by watching his dog move around the room.

An astute observer during family car trips, toddler Luke loved looking at the passing billboards on the highway, and always noticed something that his older siblings and parents missed. He learned his colors early, and preferred playing with puzzles, drawing with crayons and markers, and watching television to roughhousing or playing outside. He was the quietest sibling in the family and communicated his feelings more with his facial expressions and the pictures he drew than with his words. When he did say something, it was in very few but well-thought-out words.

Luke, like many visually talented children, has a great imagination and loves to doodle and draw, so much so that his first-grade teacher—who did a lot of oral work, talking and explaining—wrote on his report card that he was a "daydreamer" who could get more done if he concentrated more and stayed "on task." In the classroom he cannot listen for long periods without having a picture, overhead projector transparency, or outline of notes to look at; otherwise, he tunes out and finds something outside the window to gaze at, or designs a rocket or plane.

Luke gets his homework done fastest at a neat, orderly desk, and likes to have his assignments written on the board or on a sheet. He can then be quite efficient at working at it alone. He often closes his eyes or looks at the ceiling when he is memorizing or recalling information he is tested on. He depends on seeing information—in print, or on graphs, diagrams, and pictures—to learn. A good test-taker, Luke shines in math, where he can easily picture math problems and compute their answers in his head.

Like Luke, our son Christopher has visual strengths and a great visual memory. Along with that, he's blessed with a creative imagination and a wonderful ability to entertain himself. One night I went into his room to say goodnight and check on him. The lights were out, but there he lay in his bed, looking happy and busy, but with nothing to do (at least that's how it appeared to me). I asked him, "Chris, what are you doing?"

Chris said, "When I can't sleep, I work the longest, most difficult math problems I can in my mind, draw the lines, write the signs, and figure them out. Then I can relax." How much better than counting sheep!

Your child may be a strong visual learner if he or she

- ☐ uses picture clues to give him or her meaning when reading in a book.
- ☐ does chores and homework better when given a list of things to do on paper or written instructions.
- ☐ remembers faces and forgets names.
- ☐ notices details like a new picture or object in the room, his or her mom's new haircut, or a change in the classroom bulletin board.
- ☐ learns fastest and understands best if you show him or her and allow him or her to see how things are put together or how they work.
- ☐ watches others when in a social group instead of jumping into the action.

Auditory Learning: Amy

Amy, a child with auditory strengths, is a talker and a good listener. She enjoys hearing other people talk but can't wait for her turn to share ideas! Amy has a mind like a tape recorder. She remembers what you said three weeks after you said it, and then reminds you. More girls than boys have auditory and verbal strengths.

From an early age, Amy enjoyed interaction with her siblings and friends. She talked in sentences from an early age and had a colorful vocabulary. In fact, although her mother loved to hear her stories and songs, sometimes she got tired of Amy's incessant chatter and needed a quiet break! Her speech sounded like a little adult's as she related made-up stories and riddles to her family.

Even as a preschooler, she took charge and directed her playmates in "let's pretend" play. She was very vocal about her feelings and expressed herself a little dramatically. If she drew a picture, she wanted to talk about her artwork. Her favorite part of kindergarten was show-and-tell, when she could share about a new pet or happening in her family.

In the classroom, Amy is called the teacher's pet by other students because she gets called on so often. She follows oral directions easily and is quick to answer the teacher's questions. But she doesn't feel like the teacher's pet when she gets in trouble for talking too much during seat-work time. She spells everything like it sounds, so her words were sometimes written incorrectly until she started using a tape recorder to study them. She also has trouble remembering multiplication tables, which slows her down during math tests. But Amy shines in creative writing and class discussions. Like most kids with auditory strengths, she moves her lips or whispers while trying to memorize facts or spelling words for a test. She verbalizes everything and needs to hear information and then say it in order to learn it.

In addition to the above, *your child may be a strong auditory learner if he or she*

☐ is able to follow directions after listening to you once and doesn't need things repeated.

☐ likes listening to music tapes, the radio, singing, and hearing books read aloud.

☐ remembers a telephone number, zip code, or name by repeating it a few times.

☐ can maintain his or her focus just by listening in a class lecture or presentation, without having to be actively involved.
☐ benefits from a phonics approach to learning to read.
☐ solves problems by talking.

Kinesthetic or Active Learning: Karen

Karen was a very active, energetic child. She rode her bike earlier than other kids in the neighborhood and was on the go all the time. Curious and interested in everything, she learned best by doing "real-life" activities with her parents in the kitchen or manipulating things such as blocks.

Karen loved preschool, especially making animals out of clay, finger painting, and outdoor play on the equipment, balance beam, and climbing dome. She could make the most perfectly formed cow out of clay in the class, but if asked to draw a circle, her line would wander off the page. When she was four years old and the letters of the alphabet were introduced in preschool, she had a hard time distinguishing between *P* and *D*, *W* and *M*, and other letters. The letter didn't connect with the sound. So her mother, realizing that she learned physically and tactilely better than any other way, made two-and-a-half-foot-tall shapes of all the alphabet letters out of brightly colored material. Karen played with the stuffed letters, manipulated them, turned them around different ways on the floor. She actually felt how the lower-case *b* was, and if she turned it the other way, she could feel it was a *p*. Before long, she learned the alphabet letters and sounds, and was putting her big stuffed letters together to make simple words.

"We've done two things since Karen was little," said her mother, Gretchen. "One is to understand how she learns, and the other is to teach her in those ways." When she didn't seem to understand something, instead of saying "Why aren't you paying attention; how could you be so stupid?" they would think, *How are you thinking about this, Karen?* They gave Karen many opportunities for hands-on learning in her early years, which helped her master the basics and reinforced what she was learning at school. She learned math best by handling concrete objects around the house. When Gretchen was baking, she said, "Karen, let's make some cookies; show me three and a half cup measures of flour." Karen would show her the number three on her fingers, and then she measured out three cups of flour. Avid readers themselves, her parents read to her a great deal, and she became an excellent reader (way above grade level) and writer, and a straight A student. She is writing a novel on her computer and has ideas for ten different novels.

She can become easily distracted and gets overstimulated if, while trying to read a book in the room, her brother is watching sports on television. Loud music and homework don't go well together for Karen. If she loses something, she has to physically retrace her steps to find it. And if her room is a big mess, her mother needs to tell her in stages—"Pick up all your clothes"; "Now pick up all the paper"; etc.—or she becomes overwhelmed and doesn't get anything done.

Like many kinesthetically talented people, Karen is not very concerned about her physical appearance. She doesn't notice if her clothes don't match—she's too busy with projects, the computer, or taking long bike rides. She's very involved in athletics, has earned letters in all four sports at school each year, and has plenty of energy for other activities.

Children like Karen learn most effectively by *doing*—by engaging in experiments, participating in demonstrations, and when they are allowed, trying the trial-and-error method. Three-dimensional materials help them learn more than two-dimensional, pencil-and-paper, or lecture activities. They need to involve the large muscles. But school involves a lot of sitting, doing work sheets, and coloring inside little lines. Although "doers" may be very bright, they are the most at-risk group for school failure and problems (since school is mainly taught visually and auditorially). They make up the major population in "resource rooms" for learning disabled. But if they are taught in ways that capitalize on their kinesthetic and tactile strengths, *they can succeed.*

Your child may be a hands-on learner if he or she

☐ remembers best what was *done* rather than what he or she was told, read to, or talked to about.

☐ seems to learn everything by experience.

☐ tries things out and always seems to be touching things, even if they are "off-limits."

☐ needs a lot of physical contact with parents, children, and teachers, and if he or she doesn't get the positive affection—hugs, pats, etc.—will nudge, push, and pinch other classmates or siblings.

☐ is so active that shoelaces become untied and shirt tails pulled out seconds after he or she has been neatly dressed for the day.

BLENDS AND COMBINATION LEARNERS

Some people can tackle new or difficult information with two perceptual strengths. A few people have three strong modalities they use interchangeably. About 30 percent of children have what are called "mixed modalities," a blend of two or three strengths. As a preschooler, Jacob often asked to "see things" when his mother tried to explain something to him. He often played dress-up with costumes: he put his Batman costume over an elf costume, which was placed over his Frosty the Snowman costume! He was also the one in the family who would first see a jet far off in the sky or find a lost object in the grass.

Yet even as a baby, Jacob was "on the move"! He was so energetic he almost wore his parents out, broke much of what they owned from trying things out and touching, and ran away from them at every juncture—at the park, mall, or church. He always loved to work and do "big jobs" at home. He wanted to learn how to wash clothes, so his mom taught him. He can now wash whites, darks, delicates, and towels. In addition to his need to have his clothes match "just right," Jacob also enjoys this activity so much because it is meeting his kinesthetic need to be busy and productive, and to "do something."

As a preschooler, Jacob was most interested in the nursery rhymes his mom read when he could act them out. He learned them best by pretending to be Jack "jumping over the candlestick" or

Humpty-Dumpty falling off the wall.

While Jacob had excellent teachers who taught him phonics, he still learned to read primarily by sight. Once he saw a word, he usually could remember it the next time. He began reading as a kindergartner, which was a little ahead of schedule in light of a slight developmental language delay. And when he couldn't depend on his sight-word vocabulary, he had good phonics skills to rely on.

Now in the second grade, Jacob is excelling, partly because his parents understand his visual/kinesthetic learning style. Rather than preparing for tests and reviewing his schoolwork by asking questions orally, his mother often asks him to show and tell her what he has learned. Essentially it boils down to his reteaching himself the lesson.

"Five years ago I never would have known to do this," said Karen, his mother. "I just wonder where he would be and how frustrated with school he might be if I'd have insisted that he study 'just the way I learned' (by oral drill), or by silently reading over the material like his big sister does."

Jacob likes to illustrate his lesson on a dry-erase board for her. His most effective way of sharing what he learns comes from drawing, labeling, and *then* describing. In addition to making up practice tests on the computer and taking them, he often uses a "magna doodle" (a magnetic drawing board) to study. Mom asks him a potential test question or spelling word, and he writes it on the magna doodle.

He also likes using study cards. Not only is his visual sense stimulated, but his need to move is also accommodated as he shifts through the cards. He optimizes his study time by separating his cards into *know* piles and *don't know* piles. Then he concentrates on the cards that he doesn't know.

Jacob often didn't respond to his parents' verbal requests, which left them feeling frustrated. It was easy for him to get sidetracked with play or television. His mother began writing requests on yellow sticky notes and making lists of chores that needed to be done, and in record time, he now gets them done. He feels better about pleasing Mom and Dad, and about his own abilities.

COMBINING STUDY STRATEGIES

If your child has mixed modalities, combine study strategies from the chapters that best describe your child and see how they work. For example, some children are auditory/kinesthetic; they have a strong need to hear and talk about the new information, but their learning is enhanced by being able to move while memorizing or have hands-on activities. For these children, a "fill-in-the-blank" study tape (see chapter 5 on auditory learning) with a Walkman is the perfect combination. With it they can hear and practice orally but be free to march, hop, or listen in the car.

Your child may be highly visual, fairly kinesthetic and weak in auditory skills, or strong in auditory and kinesthetic and have a weak visual memory. Encourage her natural way of learning. However, all three types of learning should be developed as much as possible: A strong auditory learner should work on picturing what she hears. A visual learner should be more attentive to class lectures. A kinesthetic learner should try to *listen* and *visualize*. But all three need to write for best retention.

Whether your child is strong in learning visually, auditorially, kinesthetically, or in a combination, in the chapters that follow you will discover some strategies that will help your child capitalize on his or her strengths and learn more in the classroom and at home.

CHECKLIST FOR DISCOVERING LEARNING STRENGTHS
Read each statement and place a check in the boxes that describe your child's behavior. Then total your columns. If you checked more boxes in column A than in the other two, your child learns well visually. If you checked more in column B, he or she has auditory strengths, and if you checked mostly column C boxes, your child has kinesthetic strengths. If two columns are almost equal, your child may be a blend of learning styles.

A. Visual Strengths	B. Auditory Strengths	C. Kinesthetic Strengths
☐ Can assemble almost anything without help when using printed or pictured directions.	☐ Loves to communicate; talks a lot. ☐ In spare time, enjoys listening to CD, tape player, or radio.	☐ Hard to hold his or her attention, especially in reading, unless the story is full of action.

A. *Visual*
  Strengths

☐ Closes eyes when memorizing or remembering
☐ Very observant of details.
☐ Good at working with and solving jigsaw puzzles.
☐ In spare time, prefers to watch television or a movie, or play a video game.
☐ Likes to see what he or she is learning.
☐ Has a vivid imagination.
☐ Looking neat and wearing color-coordinated clothing is important.
☐ Can better understand things by reading about them than by listening.
☐ Is quiet; rarely volunteers answers.
☐ Thinks the best way to remember something is to picture it in his or her mind's eye.
☐ Takes many notes in a lecture.

B. *Auditory*
  Strengths

☐ Remembers television commercials, jingles, and songs after hearing once or twice.
☐ Uses rhyming words to remember names or facts.
☐ Talks aloud when working a math problem.
☐ Hears oral directions and follows them quickly.
☐ Does better in academic subjects by listening to lectures and tapes and discussing material than just reading about it.
☐ Most likely to read aloud or sub-vocalize when reading.
☐ Has difficulty reading diagrams or maps unless someone explains them to him or her.
☐ Very verbal and expressive of feelings.
☐ Good at discriminating sounds; can tell if sounds match when presented in pairs.
☐ Likes to use free time to talk to others in person or on the phone.

C. *Kinesthetic*
  Strengths

☐ Favorite pastimes include sports, active games, building things, playing outside.
☐ High-energy person; rarely sits still.
☐ As a young child, tried to touch everything he or she saw; likes to feel textures of things.
☐ Moves with music.
☐ When angry or upset shows feelings more with body language; reacts physically, like stomping out of room.
☐ Learns best what he or she can directly experience, or perform.
☐ Restless and inattentive when he or she has to sit for long periods and listen to lecture.
☐ Often uses fingers to count off items or write in the air.
☐ Tends to rumple clothing from activities.
☐ Has difficulty following and remembering oral directions.
☐ Appreciates physical affection and encouragement such as a hug or pat on the back.

_____ TOTAL A   _____ TOTAL B   _____ TOTAL C

CHAPTER FOUR

DISCOVERING YOUR OWN LEARNING STYLE

The more you can understand yourself and the way you learn, the more you can understand and help your child. As parents, we tend to expect our children to learn things the way we do. Sometimes we even want our child to match our area of strength and be a "chip off the old block."

For example, Peggy became frustrated with Eric when she told him to clean up his room, bring in his skates and soccer ball, organize his baseball cards and toys, and take out the trash, and after two hours, he had none of it done. Joanna couldn't understand why her daughter Holly didn't enjoy writing assignments the way she had in school. In fact, it puzzled her that Holly didn't like school at all. Jack was weary of explaining fractions to Jeremy for the sixth time, and still Jeremy didn't understand them.

Expecting our child to learn as we do can cause us to:

- Be happy if our child learns the same way we do and succeeds in the classroom.
- Be frustrated if he or she doesn't understand or "get it" the way we explain a problem—this causes a lot of homework

conflict and stress.

- Limit our child's learning and even bore him or her by not allowing for differences, not varying the activities and ways of presenting information (which can produce big problems for home-schooling parents teaching every subject every day).
- Be disappointed if our child with a different learning style doesn't achieve in the classroom. If he or she doesn't do well in a subject we excelled in with ease, we may think our child is lazy, stupid, or just not trying.
- Have low expectations, as manifested in a "You won't do well in math; I flunked it and you'll struggle through it, too" attitude. Because of our weakness in a subject, we may not get help for our child's learning difficulty and thus perpetuate the failure.
- Interpret the child's different learning style as misbehavior, a lack of listening, or even rebellion. The visual and auditory parent, for example, is very likely to interpret a kinesthetic learning style as mutiny. One day a dad took his teenage son out to teach him to sail. He quickly reeled off a list of instructions of how to set the sails, and then told his son to do what he had said. His son tried but could remember only two steps. Dad again repeated the instructions, this time a little louder, but his son wasn't able to complete the task. Dad got so exasperated, he threw his son overboard into the water. So much for a fun day of sailing! It took until the boy was a senior in high school before their relationship was healed.

When Brad studied, he usually ended up pacing around the dining room with his flash cards while saying his multiplication tables. To his mom, this seemed the most natural way for him to practice for tests, and she allowed it. However, when Dad got home in the evening, he complained that Brad was making noise and playing around instead of studying. *If he'd really concentrate and study as his big sister does, he'd excel, too*, Dad thought. It is vital for you to understand your learning strengths and your child's in order to help and not hinder your child's learning!

SIBLINGS LEARN DIFFERENTLY

Rarely do all children in the same family have the same way of processing information, unless they are identical twins. Fifteen-year-old identical twins Jennifer and Jessica are strongest visually: seeing and reading is their favorite way to learn things. Their secondary modality is auditory. Both like to study alone first and then ask each other questions. They excel in the same subjects—English, geography, and history—and receive generally the exact same grades on their report cards. Both play the piano, and neither are strong in sports or highly coordinated physically.

Sarah and Joanna are two-year-old fraternal twins. Sarah is very nurturing and plays with dolls constantly. Joanna is quite mechanical, changing the dials on the VCR and stereo, building towers, and sorting shapes. Sarah is more advanced in language and was more content as a baby; whereas Joanna is more active and "on the go."

Most of our children will have distinct learning styles—just as each one has a unique personality and different interests, intelligence gifts, and ways of looking at life. For instance, in the Olsen family, Wynter, thirteen years old, is a "watcher." Although strong in all modalities, her preference is visual learning. When she studies electricity, she wants to read all she can about it, do work sheets, and take the test. She excels in learning in this way. She's not interested in experiments and manipulatives because, in her own words, "They take too much time."

The Olsens' ten-year-old son, Chase, however, is a "doer"—action is his middle name. When they read the first few pages about electricity in their home school, he couldn't wait to get the wires and equipment his mom had gathered and, as the Nike commercial says, "Just do it." Chase is strongly kinesthetic in his learning style and can fix just about anything. He also can interpret complex diagrams to assemble model airplanes, which shows spatial strengths. Chase has made a burglar system, a radio, and a bell. But just reading about something leaves him cold. Because Chase and Wynter's mother understands their different learning styles, she can better motivate each of them for academic success in their home-school classroom.

When I read to my three children when they were small enough to fit on my lap, I noticed distinct differences in the way they related to reading. Chris focused in on the pictures, wanting to stay on a certain page to study a picture he was fascinated with. Justin wanted to stop to talk about the story, ask questions, and tell me what he thought about the characters. Alison, however, began to dance, sing, hop, or do whatever action the story described or suggested. Reading to all three at once was a challenge! These early reading clues gave me insight into their learning strengths: Justin, very auditory and verbal; Chris, strongly visual; and Alison, more kinesthetic/auditory.

OPPOSITES ATTRACT

Psychologists tell us that while we may feel comfortable with people like ourselves, we don't tend to marry them.[1] Opposites do attract, and husbands and wives tend to have different learning styles. For example, being more auditory and verbal in my learning style, I think primarily in words, whereas my husband, Holmes, a visual/spatial learner, thinks in pictures. And it always amazes me, the things he can picture! A whole house before he ever builds it, including all the interior detail, or even a whole neighborhood and how it could look after he developed it.

I think through many ideas at once and am happy juggling several projects at one time. Holmes thinks through one idea at a time, proceeding step by step, and does things in the proper order. I'm a "big picture" person, whereas he is a "detail" person. My desk is clean today, but when I really get going on a project—or more likely, projects—"piles" begin to stack up. They need to be visible because what's out of sight is out of mind for me! In contrast, Holmes is an orderly person who files everything away.

We all have our weaknesses, and I compensate for one of mine with that great invention, the yellow sticky note (how did we live without them?), and many long "to do" lists. Holmes, however, has a small "Day-Timer" organizer in which he writes down appointments before tucking it into his pocket or briefcase (he doesn't need to see it to remember it because he retains such a good picture of the "to do" list in his mind). I also compensate for this weakness by asking Holmes or someone nearby to remind me of interviews or appointments beforehand—and just saying it out loud helps me to remember it.

If my education and success in school had depended on my visual and spatial skills, which are needed for proficiency in sewing and assembling things from directions, I would have spent a large amount of my school day in the "resource room" for disabled learners. Even today, I could spend hours trying to assemble and sew a prom dress for Alison and end up redoing a sleeve three or more times and resorting to asking one of my visually talented friends (or Holmes) to help me through the complex parts.

Fortunately for me, school involved a lot of whole-class instruction aloud and writing, which I enjoyed, and I was blessed with teachers who explained and talked a lot. When reading, I tended to sub-vocalize, or say the words in my head, having a nice inner conversation about the new material. I talked through math story problems and was fortunate to have algebra and higher-math teachers who were expert explainers.

Although many children have to do things at school for six or eight hours that focus on their weaknesses, as adults, we don't have to. Instead, we choose jobs that enable us to function in our area of strength. We tend to avoid our weakest areas and pick careers or engage in activities in which we have some success and interest. We find then that learning style is an important factor in our vocations.

Almost all radio broadcasters I have met are auditory/verbal learners. Auditory/verbal learners also become salespeople, managers, lawyers, secondary school teachers, secretaries, speakers, and writers. They find jobs that require verbal input and interaction with other people. Kinesthetic people are attracted to jobs where they move about rather than being stuck at a desk all day. Thus they become dentists, mechanics, actors, coaches, artists, hairstylists, race car drivers, and surgeons. If they become teachers, kinesthetic learners tend to choose kindergarten teaching or a subject like drama or science. Visual parents may be teachers, computer programers and analysts, accountants, interior designers, stockbrokers, or artists.

FINDING YOUR WAY

How do you find your way around in a new city or someplace you've never been before? Directionality, or how you get your bearings and navigate in new surroundings, is a clue to how you learn best, easiest, and fastest.

We had just moved to Yarmouth, Maine, twenty miles north of Portland, and I had to go to downtown Portland occasionally to pick up Holmes or take one of the children for a doctor's appointment. I'd never driven in this city, so I knew I was in for a challenge. So how did I find my way? How would you find your way to a new place? And what do you do if you get lost? How you answer these questions reveals a lot about how you learn.

The parent with auditory strengths like me needs clearly written directions telling in words how to get to the destination. If I get lost, I prefer to stop and ask someone for directions and write it down. In fact, I enjoy chatting with folks along the way; I always learn something new or interesting. Occasionally this has backfired when the person I asked was just as much a newcomer as I was!

The visual person likes to use maps to find out how to get somewhere. Holmes and Chris are great map readers. In fact, if they've been somewhere once, they remember all the landmarks. And if they get lost, they prefer not to stop for directions but to consult the maps, keep driving, and see what went wrong.

In our first weeks in Maine, Justin, our oldest and most auditory son, took his younger brother Chris along on all his jaunts into Portland. At first we thought he simply enjoyed his company. *How nice that Justin is wanting to spend so much time with his younger brother!* I thought. But then we realized he had an ulterior motive: he knew with Christopher sitting in the front seat he'd find the ski shop, department store, or whatever he needed to.

Active doers—or kinesthetic learners—generally have a "feel" for where they're going and how to find it. That sixth sense called a good sense of direction comes in handy in a new locale. They may use a map, but if they're merely told how to get there, they'd better write it down. They figure if they get out and drive enough, they ought to be able to find the place.

HOW DO YOU MANAGE YOUR HOUSE?

Another good indicator of your learning style is how you relate to your children and spouse concerning housework, household routines, and order versus clutter. Although the following are examples of moms, the same characteristics apply to dads.

The visual parent's watchword is "a place for everything and everything in its place." Kathy, a visual mom I know, values organization above all else. Order is her middle name! She tends to be a perfectionist about how things look, especially her house. So it is well decorated, everything coordinated and very neat (no clutter out on the kitchen counter, for instance). Notes, lists, and family papers are confined to the bulletin board over the desk, never piled on it. When you walk in, it looks ready for a party.

Kathy decorated her child's room neatly with perfectly matched wallpaper and fabrics; she organized toys, games, and everything else on shelves and in special containers. She wants beds made before school every day and is easily annoyed by her child's lack of neatness in his room, which could escalate into a full-scale power struggle by the teenage years.

The house of the auditory parent, Andrea, may seem a little cluttered, but she knows where things are and can concentrate on the task at hand even with a few stacked papers or piles on her desk. She can find what she needs and likes to see projects through. Communication and relationships are a top priority to Andrea, and her hospitality and openness make her home a favorite place for kids to gather after school.

An oft-repeated phrase from her to her children is, "Let's talk about it," and she often explains to her kids how to do things and is annoyed when they don't respond right away. Often her son thinks she explains and talks too much. When problems arise, they are talked about in "family meetings." She provides her children with tape recorders and their own tapes, and is a natural storyteller. Besides reading books to her children, sharing many of her own fantasy tales and childhood recollections is a favorite pastime.

The kinesthetic parent has a sign on her refrigerator: "I'd rather have a creative mess than tidy idleness." Of the three moms, she is the least concerned with order and the least bothered by clutter, but she is also probably the most fun. Vicki is a mom actively involved with her children, using her kitchen for projects like bread making and potting new plants.

Activity is the theme of her household—rollerblades (hers and the kids'), baseballs, gloves, and bicycles are out in the driveway and yard. A basket of knitting yarn and supplies are by the couch where she's been teaching her girls to knit, and rhythm instruments lay in another corner for impromptu music times. Vicki loves to take her children to the park and gets physically involved with them by running, swinging, and dancing around the living room when a favorite, lively song plays on the stereo. In fact, she participates on an adult soccer team on Saturdays, and works out at the YMCA whenever she can.

An orderly, clean house takes a back seat to activity and time together with the children. All this fun is wonderful if her husband isn't a visual perfectionist whose main priority is order and who doesn't mind stepping over the latest project or a mini-trampoline sitting out on the living room floor.

A PARENT WITH MIXED MODALITIES

Perhaps you can't relate to only one style, but fit somewhere in between these descriptions and possess a combination of strengths, like my friend Diane, who is a visual/kinesthetic parent. Her lucky kids—the best of two styles is reflected in her parenting and household.

Although Diane loves beautiful colors and interesting furniture and collectibles in her home, the mood is flexible rather than structured, and people are more important to her than perfection. "We're always working on projects," says Diane. "Like last Friday, Charlie was out of school for teachers' conferences. We worked on collages with a variety of textures and paints on the dining room table." Diane's hobby and part-time business is making original clay creations; she has a kiln in the garage to fire them. She also collects interesting things. Her boys like to make things, too. "Not structured crafts," says Diane, "but I always give them a lot of paint, clay, etcetera, and let them put things together and make what they want to." Her kinesthetic strengths show in how she's not afraid to try different things. Always experimenting, she doesn't follow plans for a craft or clay creation but works and plays with it until it "feels" right.

Diane is outdoorsy and adventurous—her family camps, hikes, fishes, and bikes together. And her real love is working in the colorful cutting garden that takes up three-fourths of their front yard.

LEARNING SOMETHING NEW

The last and most important way to get a handle on your learning style as a parent is to think about how you would learn a new piece of complicated technology from the ground up if you were under some time pressure and your performance on the equipment mattered in your next job evaluation. How would you want to go about learning skills for a new computer?

I have just gotten a new IBM-compatible computer because my good old 1983 Panasonic Word Processor (a wonderful machine I've never had to repair in ten years of heavy use) is now a dinosaur. Worst of all, it is not compatible with any magazine editors' or publishers' computers. Since I have to deliver manuscripts on a disk that's compatible with their computers, I was compelled to go "high tech" and now am staring at a computer I know nothing about, a manual full of directions that are Greek to me, and a looming deadline.

Am I going to muddle through the thick manual to figure out how to use it? Not if I can help it! Would I like to use the tutorial and figure it out as I go along? On my own, this would not be effective.

But if I can call my brother George long distance for some phone consultation, during which I can ask questions when I get stuck, that might work. I'm a "tell me, show me, and most important, let me ask questions and clarify what I'm doing" learner. And the more foreign the task, the more I need not only to see it but also to hear it, say it, and do it. I saw an ad for a training class—a crash course where not only would I have a tutorial on the computer screen but also a trainer to help if I got stuck. I thought that was for me, but when I got there, I found the tutorial on the computer was the main teacher and the trainer didn't want to be bothered. I learned what I could. When I learned the most, however, was when Donna, a friend who is a computer expert, came over and explained many features of my computer, demonstrated them to me, and answered my questions. What a great help she was.

What about you? Would you read the manual and look at the many diagrams to figure out how to use the computer? (If this is your preference, you have visual strengths.) In fact, Donna's favorite books to read are computer manuals! Would your approach be "Let me fiddle with the computer and figure this out," until you had it mastered? (You probably have kinesthetic strengths.) Or would you, like me, prefer to have someone explain the operation of the machine to you—a primarily auditory and verbal method? Maybe you would want to combine methods.

Following is a summary of some of the behaviors endemic to the three learning types in parents:

Kinesthetic "Doer" Parents

- Are quick to give hugs, pats on the back, and physical affection.
- Tend to be involved in sports, working out, or keeping fit.
- Show their emotions by their body language or actions.
- Discipline their child by picking the child up or other physical action.
- Don't like to sit for long PTA meetings or lectures.

Auditory "Talker" Parents

- Discipline by telling the child what he or she has done wrong and explaining what he or she needs to do next time.
- Do a lot of encouraging, praising, and explaining to the child.
- Like listening to the radio, music, or tapes.
- Show emotions by voice tone (sometimes unpleasantly shrill if really upset) and by words.
- Like to sit close to the middle in a seminar so they can comment to their neighbors about what is said without disturbing the speaker.

Visual "Watcher" Parents

- Are quiet and don't say much when they are upset, but the children can tell by their facial expressions that they are really ticked off or perhaps sad.
- Like reading, movies, and television.
- Discipline by giving "that look" or insisting the child have "timeout" in his or her room.
- Like to sit close in a movie or up front in a seminar so they can see the speaker.

Now you should have a good idea of what your learning style is and where your strengths are. This will help you better understand your child's learning differences as we look at how to identify your child's learning style in the next chapters. You will also be able to eliminate many homework hassles and conflicts, and encourage the success of each child in your family, regardless of how he or she learns.

CHAPTER FIVE

TALKERS AND LISTENERS
AUDITORY LEARNING

W hen Brittany was barely two years old, she would repeat word for word what her mother said. One day her mom, in her first few months of pregnancy, was lying on the couch, very tired after an excursion to the grocery store, post office, and mall with her daughter. Brittany wanted her to play, and Liz said, "I can't, honey. I'm totally exhausted, and you know when I get exhausted, I just have to rest."

When Brittany's dad got home, he said, "Let's go to the park."

Brittany replied, "I can't, Daddy. I'm totally exhausted, and you know when I get exhausted, I just have to rest!" This repetition was an everyday occurrence. Needless to say, they had to be very careful about what they said within Brittany's earshot!

Brittany also was fascinated with the sound and meaning of words. She asked what the names of objects were continually. She asked about all kinds of words she heard spoken, read, or on television or radio—little and big. One day she asked, "What were you doing, Mommy?"

Her mom said, "I was imitating the cat."

Two-and-a-half-year-old Brittany asked, "What does 'imitate' mean?" Then she immediately began using the word. She also remembers songs heard in a movie only once and can sing them with the correct words and rhythm days or weeks later. Brittany has a sharp and sensitive tape recorder inside her mind taking note of everything she hears!

Now five years old, she's also the family's chatterbox, talking constantly from the time her eyes open until she falls asleep. As much as her mother delights in her expressiveness, she sometimes tires of her talking and looks forward to the quiet of late evening when the children are in bed. But even at bedtime, Brittany chats with her baby sister in her crib and stuffed teddy bears and rabbits on the bed. She loves her series of Disney books with audiotapes and plays them over and over. Brittany enjoys drawing and art activities, but if given a choice will select musical activities, listening and singing along with tapes or the radio.

As a four-year-old, Brittany surprised her grandparents and family friends by memorizing a whole chapter of the Bible to say at a church talent night, and the same night sang a song with her dad. She has memorized other poems and long passages, and she absorbs words like a sponge. Even when she was a toddler, it was hard for her mom to hurry up a book if they were short of time, because if she would miss a word, Brittany would say, "No, that's not how it goes," and say what was on the page. After being read the story only a few times, she'd memorized it word for word. Her inner recorder worked fast and retained the information well.

This strong auditory learner with language talent will enjoy many aspects of school. Already at five years old, Brittany is the first one to answer every question in kindergarten and other group classes. Mentally processing the teacher's questions and verbalizing the answer is fun for her, and she can do it faster than anyone else in the class. She enjoys listening—to a point. But if she has to sit still and the teacher talks the whole class period, she finds the lack of interaction boring and likes to join in the talking. Children of this age still need movement and activity, and she is no exception. But Brittany will need to learn some patience and self-control—waiting for her turn to talk—and become an even better listener as she grows and begins formal schooling in a classroom situation.

Many academic situations are auditory, so in many classrooms this type of learner does well. When the teacher instructs and gives the class verbal directions, has class discussions on a regular basis, and asks questions to clarify the content, the student with verbal strengths has an advantage. Thus a talker/listener with an auditory bent like Brittany will show many strengths in school. He or she will

- Follow oral instructions after listening only once, and won't need to hear things over and over.
- Do well in tasks requiring phonetic analysis.
- Learn to read most effectively with a phonics approach.
- Sequence speech sounds well.
- Love the read-aloud time of the school day.
- Perform well verbally; do well with relating ideas and storytelling.
- Grasp concepts quickly.
- Enjoy music class, drama, and role-playing opportunities.
- Do well in expressing himself or herself in written communication.
- Appear brighter than test scores show him or her to be.[1]

The talker/listener may also become frustrated by weaknesses that show up in the classroom, such as having difficulty with silent reading and spelling. In addition, auditory learners have a need for clear verbal explanations when given new or difficult material to learn, even if it's in a textbook, on a work sheet, or on the board. They can also become very distracted by noise in the classroom or in the hall, and their love for talking to classmates can become a problem.

Brittany is like many children I've seen who are very bright but may not do well in school unless their parents and teachers understand and capitalize on their strengths, thus allowing them to perceive and understand the information, retain it, and be able to apply it.

You see, you can't memorize what you don't understand. If, for instance, your child can't comprehend math concepts by merely looking at numbers on a work sheet, you could demonstrate with beans, by cutting a straw into sections, or some other concrete method, and then discuss the concept and have your child put the ideas into his or her own words. If a chapter of history or science is difficult to comprehend through silent reading, ask your child to read it aloud or into a tape recorder.

What's important is to help your child understand the concepts and information by introducing them through his or her strength, and then transferring the information from *short-term memory* to *long-term memory* with some creative study strategies. Short-term memory holds information, words, or numbers just as long as they are before the class or as long as the student actively thinks about them. But once information moves into a child's long-term memory, it can be brought out, recalled, and applied to a test, or a real-life problem or activity.

How does the information go from short-term memory to long-term memory? Repetition is necessary, but it doesn't have to be boring and tedious. The best learning takes place when we use the child's strengths rather than weaknesses in the practice and drill. Just reading multiplication tables over and over ($2 \times 1 = 2$, $2 \times 2 = 4$, etc.) may be boring to a child who is verbally oriented and needs to hear and say—or maybe even sing—the times tables. Just oral practice or a lecture is boring to the active child who needs a hands-on approach. The more we make the repetition lively and active for the kinesthetic learner by bouncing a basketball, playing a game, or writing on a big chalkboard, the better he or she remembers the information.

According to Dr. Rita Dunn, the best approach for maximum learning is to start with your child's strongest perceptual strength, reinforce it with his or her secondary modality, and finally, use the new information in a creative way. For the creative part, for example, she suggests: "Ask students to make up a poem with states and capitals, or to make up a game. They might write a letter explaining states and capitals to a child in another country. Any real creative application works, and you will not believe the kind of achievement gains."[2]

Let's look at some strategies for learning auditorially—with listening, talking, rehearsing, taping, role-playing, and other strategies.

STUDYING IN STYLE

One night our daughter Alison had thirty irregular verb forms to memorize—present, past, and past perfect tenses—ninety words in all. She had missed the explanation, drill, and practice in class due to illness, so at first the task looked overwhelming. I went over the list orally with her, having her say the words. Then I showed her how to make a tape recording of each verb and its forms. Alison enjoyed making the tape and then played it over several times, reciting along with the tape until the sounds were firmly fixed in her mind. She was seeing the words, hearing them, and saying them, which made a stronger imprint on her memory. I gave her a practice test I had written out before bedtime, circling the verbs she missed, and she studied those words, saying them aloud. The whole study session took approximately forty-five minutes.

The next morning, Alison got her tape recorder out while she was dressing and practiced the verb forms again. That day, she made an A on the test and came home with greatly boosted confidence and motivation. She needed to practice hearing and saying the information to do her best and began to use tape-recording to study for geography, French, and other subjects.

"When does a learning style become a learning deficit or disability?" I asked my friend Steve, a psychologist.

"For me," he said, "it happens when you don't let me use my auditory strengths! That's the way I've always learned best."

So, too, with children who have auditory and verbal strengths. Let's capitalize on these strengths, help them take a different approach when they have to master new or difficult information, and watch them achieve. Here's how:

Make Your Own Study Tape

A blank tape and tape recorder is a wonderful study tool for children with auditory strengths. Kinesthetic learners enjoy using it too, especially if they can listen to the tape with a Walkman and move around during their oral practice.

First, have the child make flash cards out of index cards (with questions on one side and answers on the other). To make the tape, the student asks a question into the microphone, waits five or more seconds, and then goes on to the next question. After the tape is made, the child plays it back and inserts the answer after each question. This boosts understanding and memory, as the child sees the fact, says it, and hears it. The study-tape method can be used in any subject, from simple addition facts and multiplication tables to French vocabulary and states and capitals.

Tape-recording chapters of textbooks, class notes, and lectures also helps the verbal learner master the material. It can also aid reading comprehension. When Joseph read silently, he didn't comprehend his history or literature. His mom had him read his work into a tape recorder and then play it back to himself. By doing this, his grades came up a letter in each subject.

Even for older students, tape-recording is useful. Although Ann is a good student in her first year of law school, she finds that when she tape-records her twenty-page outline of notes on each course before the final and then plays it back several times, she makes higher grades and has better overall mastery.

Sherry, a home-schooling mother, makes a daily tape of instructions for the day's lessons for her daughter Laura. She can slow the tape down or listen to it again if she needs to. For example, Sherry reads the phonics rule on the tape, gives Laura several examples, tells her which page to turn to in the workbook, and includes specific encouragement—"I know you know this part; let's go over it one more time." Then she goes on to the math instructions and other subjects for the day. This has enabled Laura to be more independent and yet have clear directions in her home study.

Tape-recording shouldn't totally replace oral instruction. A short time spent asking the child questions and having the child answer them out loud can be multiplied back in the retention and understanding gained. It also helps you keep in touch with what your child is learning and provides a springboard for discussion of the topic.

Set Information to a Familiar Tune

For example, to help your child remember the vowels, sing "Old MacDonald's Farm" like this: "Old MacDonald had a farm—A, E, I, O, U." Auditory learners and kids with a musical bent especially enjoy this way of learning. Whether it is an algebra formula, dates in history, or Spanish vocabulary words, music helps all learners remember important information. "I learned the Preamble of the Constitution by singing it," said a teacher I know. "My friends memorized it visually but I sang it. When we had to write it on our test, I sang it quietly to myself and wrote the words down as I sang. I made one-hundred percent and had total recall on that portion of the government test."

Setting information to a tune is also useful for memorizing math facts and spelling words. Most children are entertained by music, and music-related activities hold their attention longer than activities without music. Even more important, music stimulates right-brain activity, while speech is a left-brain activity. When the two are combined, you've greatly strengthened learning and memory.

Researchers and therapists have found that even when people have lost the ability to speak, they can learn all over again when phrases are set to music.[3] Whether it is verbal information or numbers, music helps with recall and retrieval.

Poetry

The rhythm and rhyme of poetry works in a similar way to aid memory, especially for auditory learners. In phrases such as "In fourteen hundred and ninety-two Columbus sailed the ocean blue" and "Thirty days has September, April, June, and November. All the rest have thirty-one, except February, which has twenty-eight, or in leap year, twenty-nine," we learned valuable information and can recall it years later. "*I* before *e* except after *c* or when sounded as *a* as in *neighbor* and *weigh*" came in handy to spell many words correctly.

When I was in ninth grade, we were to create a poster that illustrated an algebraic concept. I drew a garden with bright flowers (each had an algebra formula inside) and a sun-bonneted girl watering them with her tilted-over watering can. The verse I made up went like this:

Mary, Mary, quite contrary
How do your polynomials subtract?
You change the sign of the subtrahend,
Then add as a matter of fact.

Although I've forgotten a lot of other algebra over the years, through lack of use, I haven't forgotten that formula, the verse, or the picture. Help your child develop songs or poems to remember the fifty states, the multiplication tables, or other information. If your child can help come up with the words and/or melody, and add a picture, he or she will remember it better. The child can tape-record the song or poem for more reinforcement.

Learn with Both Sides of the Brain

To say someone is totally right-brained or left-brained is an over-simplification. We all use both sides of the brain in learning and working on a day-to-day basis. But just as we have a tendency to use one hand or foot more than the other, most people's thinking favors one hemisphere of the brain. The left side functions mainly in analyzing incoming data in a logical, sequential way, and decoding and interpreting language. The right side functions in creative processes, mental images, emotions, and music, to name a few. The right hemisphere is involved with thinking for visual and spatial tasks. The left processes in a step-by-step way, while the right tends to process all at once, looking for patterns and connecting things into a whole.

"By using the whole brain approach," says Dr. Wanda Draper, psychiatrist and professor at the University of Oklahoma Medical School, "you are using the right hemisphere to map out or illustrate what the left hemisphere has reasoned or deduced."[4] She and other experts maintain that when you use these two hemispheres together you increase your thinking capacity, understanding, and retention.

One practical way to learn with both sides of the brain (combining the verbal and visual) simultaneously is by using clustering as a pre-writing activity. For example, before I have my students write a poem about summer, we make a visual picture on the board with the word *summer* in a circle, and lines going out to other circles that we fill with different sensory words. We brainstorm orally as a class to generate ideas for the outer circles. One circle contains smells of summer (the charcoal smell of hamburgers cooking on the grill, the chlorine bleach smell of the swimming pool, etc.). One circle contains tastes of summer (delicious chocolate ice cream, juicy watermelon, and many more!), then sounds, feelings, sights, and colors.

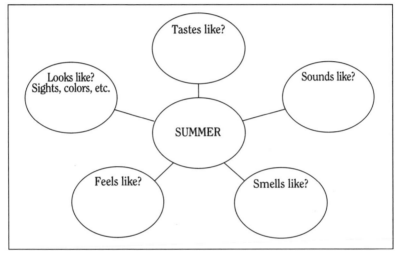

Following the group clustering activity, each student takes the cluster he or she has drawn on paper and writes a poem about summer. In combining the language activity (left-brained function) with the visual activity (right-brained function), the ideas are multiplied and students come up with images they would not think of if just told to "write a poem about summer." The creative clusters and poems that emerge are amazing, both from the class as a whole and from individual students.

Other subjects involve left and right processing. Math, for example, is very step by step in solving problems and analytical (left). But it also uses right-brained functions in finding patterns and estimating.

Another example of two-sided learning would be to draw diagrams, maps, and charts to represent concepts or stick figures to represent historical characters as a part of note-taking in a class lecture or a home-study session. Picture what you are studying while asking yourself: What are the key words and ideas? Why are they important to the main topic?[5]

Enhancing Visual Abilities

Very verbal/auditory people often do not rely on visual abilities. They may not even be aware of seeing pictures in their mind's eye, and may need practice generating pictures. They need to be challenged, however, to develop visual capacities because these thinking skills provide great help (and save time) in remembering many different kinds of information in certain areas—such as math facts and formulas, spelling words, geography, geometry, and history.

Just as listening skills are needed to excel in the classroom and in real-life job situations, making pictures is a helpful tool for much academic learning as well. After drawing a time line or a chart of the planets and their characteristics, the child should verbalize it and discuss the concepts and connections.

In spelling, for instance, you can't spell a word correctly from how it smells, tastes, or even sounds. A lot of words just don't sound like they look. The student needs an accurate picture in his or her mind of how the word looks. So here's a method that helps auditory learners remember spelling words:

1. Look at the word and say it. Spell each letter aloud.
2. Close your eyes and think what the word looks like. Ask, "Can you picture it?"
3. Say it, while looking at the chalkboard in your mind, and try to spell it.
4. Open your eyes, look at the word, and check your spelling.

You can also cover the word and write it several times, then close your eyes and try to spell the word aloud correctly. In this way, the student is making pictures and attaching the sound to the word. Then when the teacher calls out the word on a test and the student is expected to write it correctly, the student hears it, the picture comes up, and he or she can copy it down.

A good method for learning lines of poetry or speeches is to write the sentence on the board. Have the student say the verse or sentence aloud. Erase one word and have him or her say the sentence and try to picture the words in his or her mind's movie screen. Repeat, erasing another word. Continue in the same way until all the words are gone. Have the child say it in its entirety and check with the original sentence.

Combining modalities in these ways—especially verbal and visual—enhances learning and remembering. In several studies, M. C. Wittrock of the UCLA Graduate School of Education has shown that students recall information and words better when a verbal *and* visual activity is used. He demonstrated that students remembered vocabulary words better when they read the definitions and drew their own pictures to represent them than when they merely read the words and wrote the definitions. He also taught kinetic molecular theory (which is extremely complex) to kindergarten and elementary children using pictures, concrete examples, and verbal explanation. All concepts were represented visually. With concrete examples, the children could relate to and connect with something they were familiar with. The results were impressive! Almost 70 percent of the children learned and remembered the concepts a year after the experiment.[6]

In the chapter on visual learning I will demonstrate more visual methods such as mapping and diagramming techniques for learning information.

Mnemonics

Mnemonics are techniques to improve the memory, or "memory aids," such as acrostics. Just like any other part of the body, the memory gets better the more we *exercise* it. One good way to exercise the memory is to make an acrostic. An acrostic allows you to remember a list of words by taking the first letter from each word and substituting another word beginning with that same letter. For example:

Africa...............Aunt
Asia.................Alice
Australia...........Ate
Antarctica ....Apples
North America ....Nearly
Europe.............Every
South America....Sunday

Thus, the sentence "Aunt Alice ate apples nearly every Sunday" serves as a reminder for the names of the continents.

Acronyms are another mnemonic aid. To memorize a list of words using an acronym, take the first letter of each word and make a new word from each of those letters. Here's a familiar one for the names of the Great Lakes:

H—Huron
O—Ontario
M—Michigan
E—Erie
S—Superior

As one educator said, "There are no poor memories, only poor learning habits!" Memory is vastly improved by using strategies to organize the information—thus moving the information from short-term to long-term memory (the brain's file cabinet). You can remember the elements of a short story by the acronym SCAT (setting, characters, action, theme) or the order of scientific classification by "King Phillip came over for green spaghetti" (kingdom, phylum, class, order, family, genus, species). If your child or a study group makes up the acrostic, it is even more effective, and the sillier and more humorous, exaggerated, or colorful, the better. A chain of silly words that forms a sentence works the same way. Some students made up the following:

■ "Never eat sour wieners" for the directions north, east, south, west.

- "Dad made sweet bread" for the steps in division: divide, multiply, subtract, and bring down.
- "Nancy picks very ample apples if canning properly" for the eight parts of speech: noun, pronoun, verb, adverb, adjective, interjection, conjunction, preposition.

Mnemonics can be made up in any subject: language arts, math, science, social studies. These can help your child remember the colors of the spectrum, the names of the planets, or the order of the metric system: "King Henry doesn't milk dairy cows Monday" (K-kilo, H-hecta, D-deca, M-meter, D-deci, C-centi, M-milli).

The Concentration Card Game

This game improves visual memory, which often needs improvement in auditory learners. It also provides a good chance for interaction and going over the questions orally. For this game, all the questions and answers are written on one side of colored blank cards—the question on one card, the answer on another—and then randomly placed facedown on the floor or table. The first player turns over two cards, trying to match a question with the correct answer. If the player gets a match, he or she gets to keep the cards and is rewarded with another turn. If the player turns over mismatched cards, he or she returns the cards, facedown, to the same position on the floor or table, and the next player takes a turn. The play continues until all the cards have been matched together. The player with the most cards at the end wins.

Students can make board games of all kinds with the information they are assigned, with great results. They get reinforcement through writing the spaces on the board or making the cards, oral practice as the answers are shared, interaction with other learners, and a fun way to study.

Post-it notes (also called sticky notes) for visual reminders in textbooks, notebooks, and desk areas at home and school will trigger memory of what needs to be done or of key concepts and can be a helpful aid to auditory learners.

Facilitating Writing Assignments

To facilitate writing assignments, especially if your child has difficulty getting started or writer's block on an assigned theme or essay, begin by brainstorming about the topic and writing the ideas in cluster form with the idea in the middle and connecting thoughts written around it like spokes on a wheel. Rehearsing, or talking through the ideas, is one of the best pre-writing strategies for the auditory learner.

If the assignment is a personal-experience story, your child could tape-record the experience as he or she remembers it, then play the tape back and fill in missing details or rearrange events in chronological order, writing them down. After the written narrative has gotten "cold"—that is, put away for a few hours or a day—have your child read aloud the story, revise, add missing details, and edit. A quick-find word guide (or spell-check on a word processor) can be used to check and correct the spelling of words.

Math Strategies

Let the student make auditory tapes of story problems in addition to the written-down problem or accompanying picture. In addition, writing in math can be helpful to verbal students. They can write their own story problem that involves addition, multiplication, and subtraction. Or they can write an addition problem that equals a given answer, like 555, for example. Rewriting an assigned story problem in their own words clarifies the thought processes and helps students come up with a problem-solving strategy.

Clustering can be used in math to represent and organize information to be learned. To review and prepare for a test on fractions, for example, the student and his or her study-partner learning group could brainstorm and discuss everything they know about fractions. One student writes "FRACTIONS" in the middle of a big sheet of paper. Around it the student then writes information such as "Ways to write fractions," followed by a list of these ways; "Ways fractions are used and applied in real world," followed by a list; and "Functions you can do with fractions" (addition, subtraction, division, multiplication, reducing, etc.).[7] Writing in math is a great way to boost comprehension of concepts and retention.

Students can also describe things in words, like a geometric shape: "A rectangle has four sides and its corners are all right angles." Then they try to "see" what they have described in words. Students need not only to see the problem worked on the board but also to hear the teacher talk through the problem-solving process.

Reading Material Aloud

Reading material aloud, whatever the age of the auditory/verbal student, is helpful. It aids in clarifying ideas and enables the student to get a "big picture" and a better understanding of the concepts. Ask the student to read a chapter aloud of history, science, or whatever is assigned. You could alternate—parent reads a paragraph or page, then student reads a paragraph or page. Even if just the first few pages of a chapter are read aloud and discussed briefly in this way, it will increase comprehension of the material.

Study Groups

A home study group before a big test or exam is invaluable, especially for junior high and high school students. The best study groups have a few hardworking classmates who want to do well on the test. In saying the information aloud in their study group, they'll understand it better. They will inspire each other's efforts and stir up a little competition. They can orally go over the material; discuss ideas, key words, and concepts; and quiz each other. Then each one tries to figure out the questions the teacher will ask, writes them down, pools them together into a practice test, and takes it.

Studying for Tests

Here's a good strategy for studying a chapter in a textbook, from the time the chapter is first assigned to the final test. First, have your child listen in class, taking good notes and tape-recording the lecture if the teacher allows it. The auditory learner will get more out of reading the chapter *after* the class presentation. That night, the child reads the chapter (aloud if desired), reviews class notes, and discusses information with a study partner or you or your spouse.

During the next day's study period, the child should review notes and reinforce material with his or her secondary modality—by a visual method (like drawing a cluster or learning web of the main concepts and their connections) or a kinesthetic method (saying the information while throwing Nerf baskets or teaching the material to the family on a chalkboard). The student could make flash cards on index cards and make a study tape with them, or use a more active method (see chapter 6).

The last night before the test is time for *review:* have your child replay the tape of the class lecture or study tape and go over questions orally with someone. Then have him or her do something creative with the information (like write a letter explaining the concepts to a friend or make up a game, for example). By going over the material for four days, the child will process the information into his or her long-term memory and can then retrieve it when needed to excel on the test, but also to apply and use weeks or months later.[8]

A Quiet Place to Study

In home study sessions, provide a reasonably quiet place to study. Most auditory learners tend to be distracted by noises. Help your child stay organized—by writing down assignments in each class, keeping a calendar of activities and tasks that demand his or her time—and give plenty of feedback on homework, classwork, and tests that are sent home.

Auditory learners are encouraged more by positive words, genuine recognition of improvement, and occasional praise than other children. Watch the messages you deliver daily! The things we say to auditory learners are recorded on their sensitive inner tape players, stored indefinitely, and replayed. Whether it's "You can do this math assignment. Look how many more problems you got right this week!" or "I had trouble in math and hated it; it wouldn't surprise me if you did, too," or "We love and appreciate you—you're a joy to us," or "You can't do anything right," the messages become the self-talk that plays again and again—at school during class time and test-taking, at home while studying—and hinders or boosts motivation.

For the best methods for learning to read for the auditory child, see chapter 8, and for more ways to bypass weaknesses and ensure success at school, see chapter 11, "Your Child in the Classroom."

ENHANCING AUDITORY LEARNING IN PRESCHOOLERS

The foundations we build before children start first grade are vitally important. Readiness for reading and language building and foundations for math skills all take place in the preschool years. Provide your child with many opportunities for storytelling and books, read-aloud times, records, tapes of the spoken words (stories), and music. Your child will enjoy the sounds of words, things with rhymes, alliteration, and onomatopoeia. Talk with your child as much as possible and encourage curiosity by answering questions enthusiastically (which can be hard after the fiftieth question of the day!). In addition, here are some ways to enhance auditory learning:

Preschool Activities
What Doesn't Belong?
Name four objects like a kitty, bird, hat, and dog. Have your child listen, and then ask, "Which thing doesn't belong here?" Then list a different group of things—a jacket, table, glove, and sock—and repeat the question, "What doesn't belong?"

I Spy
Each player, in turn, looks around the room (or car or outside) and says, "I spy something *green*." The other players attempt to identify the "something." The one who guesses correctly gets to be the spy on the next turn.

Write Your Own Story
Set out photographs of your child and your family. Ask your child to make up a story about each picture and write it down as he or she is dictating. When your child is finished, read the story aloud, tape-recording it, and then bind it together with yarn or staples into a book.

Fill in the Story
Read your child a story, occasionally saying "ditto" instead
of a word in the story. Ask your child to fill in a word that he
or she thinks will work in the context of the sentence.
Example: "There once was a boy with a little toy *ditto* with a
rat-a-tat-tat. ..."

In the next chapter we'll look at kinesthetic learners, their
strengths, and strategies to help them learn and achieve.

Chapter Six

DOERS AND TOUCHERS
Kinesthetic Learning

One day when he was five, Aaron spent the afternoon at his grandmother's house. While she made a quick trip to the grocery store, he was supposed to be playing with his cars. But when she returned and walked by the living room, she realized her prize figurine's arms and legs were broken off.

"Why did you do this?" Aaron's grandmother asked. "You've broken my antique figurine!"

"I just wanted to see if the arms moved. I wanted to see if the legs moved or if it would bend," Aaron said. Inquisitive Aaron had no intention of causing a problem or ruining anything. He was just a "doer" and "toucher" through and through.

The way Aaron and other kinesthetic-tactile kids learn often gets them into trouble. Just like Thomas Edison, who while trying to imitate birds, once sat on the nest of eggs and smashed them all. Aaron's hands-on way of finding out how things work also meant dismantling the remote-control car he got at Christmas and taking apart Mom's toaster when it wouldn't pop the toast up. However, he did put it back together and even fixed it! Although he's now the best swimmer on the YMCA swim team and a gymnast who has already won several youth competitions, Aaron is restless when he has to sit for long periods in his desk doing pencil-and-paper seat work, and has been assigned to the low reading group for second grade.

After Cary's teacher taught the science class about cell division, assigned a chapter to read in the textbook, and a work sheet to finish, Cary read through everything and still didn't understand. Her first quiz grade on the material was only a sixty, not enough to pass. That week her tutor pulled out some clay and actually made a model of a cell while explaining and demonstrating the difference between animal and plant cell division. Then she let Cary show and explain the concepts of cell division using the clay. She let her use a pen to mark the chromosomes. When her mom picked her up at the end of the tutoring session, Cary showed her the cell and told her what she had learned. Usually she had trouble explaining what she'd learned, but with the three-dimensional clay cell, she communicated it clearly and glowed with pride. And her grade on the chapter test rose to a B.

Lauree was not interested in the chapter on the human body until she got to dissect a chicken. When her mom turned the material into a hands-on approach and she got to feel the muscles, identify the bones by touch, and then write them down, the subject came alive to her.

Her older brother John said, "Oh, gross!" while she cut into the chicken. He'd rather just read about it and write a report. But Lauree's active curiosity was engaged by the dissection. She also loves to put together "potions" from the kitchen and see what happens in the chemical reactions. When reading, she gets distracted easily. And when they read aloud as a family, they've found that she concentrates and enjoys the story or chapter much more when she can do something with her hands, such as draw a picture of what they are reading about.

Children with kinesthetic and tactile strengths are active, hands-on learners. "Kinesthetic" means learning things best by doing them; they like their whole body to be involved in the learning activity. "Tactile" means learning is enhanced by touching and manipulating equipment or material. Sometimes students are both tactile and kinesthetic, but not always. Since the study methods that follow in this chapter generally work just as well for both kinds of active learners, I will refer to them interchangeably.

Students like Lauree, Cary, and Aaron are the most at risk for frustration at school and home because the majority of instruction, and many of the tasks and testing, are auditory and visual—it's not because they aren't bright. Their strengths are in the kinesthetic area. Their high energy levels often try our patience. Their difficulty with abstract concepts challenges our teaching methods. But they have tremendous potential and intelligence, if we just learn how to teach them, show them how to capitalize on their strengths, and compensate for their weaknesses.

Sometimes just a modification of a study strategy will make the difference. Steven caught on to the math functions and mastered his math facts rapidly when his mom supplemented his math instruction with Touch Math (a tactile way of teaching math). (See appendix, pages 192, for address and toll-free phone number.) Cary's tutor has her write her mnemonics in salt to increase her retention. "If I just have her say aloud the acrostic 'Can Cherry speak?' for three types of clouds—cirrus, cumulus, and stratus—she forgets it, but when she writes it in salt, she can get it right on the test and remember it the next week." Capitalizing on her kinesthetic strengths has boosted not only her grades but also her self-esteem.

A kinesthetic learner may be strong in the following:

- Fine and gross motor balance (or may be better at gross, or large muscle, coordination and balance)
- Rhythmic movement
- Identifying and matching objects
- Taking gadgets apart and putting them back together again
- Using concrete objects as learning aids
- Three-dimensional thinking
- Creativity, problem solving, and seeing the connection between ideas

The computer in these children's brains keeps their movements timed perfectly in a diving performance or crucial soccer kick. They have excellent motor memory. They enjoy doing things with their hands, touch everything in their path, write things over and over, and get up and walk around frequently in a classroom. Thus they may be the first picked for the baseball team but not the teacher's pet! They are the best and fastest at cutting out cardboard letters for the class bulletin board, and they manipulate puzzles and other materials well. But they may have difficulty counting by rote or sequencing materials without concrete objects to count, and learning abstract symbols such as letters or math symbols is difficult without manipulatives or real-life experiences.

Albert Einstein said, "Knowledge is experience—everything else is just information." How can we encourage and facilitate the learning of these bright hands-on kids?

HANDS-ON LEARNING

"Rather than fight their natural learning style, why not use it to help them uncover the patterns in the universe?" asks Elaine Gaines, learning specialist and author of the Math Alive program. "The real world, tangible things, hands-on stuff are the 'textbooks and work sheets' of mathematics for children," she adds. Elaine feels that mathematics education in America has sunk to an all-time low level because our children are inundated with math work sheets, workbooks, and textbooks and are made to memorize masses of information that mean nothing to them because from ages five to twelve children learn and think concretely rather than abstractly.[1]

This problem applies to all children, but especially to those who have kinesthetic strengths and a three-dimensional thinking style. With just pencil-and-paper activities, their learning and motivation plummet. Research from learning centers and neurologists shows that many people with great intelligence in the three-dimensional realm—the world-renowned designer of prostheses or the engineer, actor, inventor, or Olympic gold-medal winner—have trouble with two-dimensional academic tasks (like deciphering printed words, numbers, and symbols in textbooks and on work sheets).[2] These children learn best when they touch, see, hear, *and* experience real-life things. For example, the concept of one-third will be best understood and internalized after they divide one candy bar into three parts; the symbol $.20, by counting two out of ten dimes for the savings bank; or by counting three leaves on five clovers to demonstrate $3 \times 5 = 15$ leaves.[3]

If we can use hands-on learning methods at the highest levels of education, such as medical school and graduate-school research, why can't we use them during the crucial elementary years when it matters the most?[4] The more schools can return to hands-on instruction, the more children will achieve. Provide buttons, packages of sticks, muffin cups, and beans for counting and performing math functions. Have firsthand experiments when studying electricity, insects, or other science areas. Dissect flowers and then label the parts. Get a frog hatchery kit, an ant farm, or a Science-by-Mail problem-solving kit in which your child gets to correspond with a scientist.[5]

Go from the concrete to the concept and then to the abstract (figuring the problem out on paper). Let's apply this principle of hands-on learning to other tasks kinesthetic students must tackle. For when we do—as Gretchen did when she made the stuffed alphabet letters her daughter Karen could feel, play, and spell with, and when she encouraged her to measure and count while helping her cook in the kitchen—we find they can excel and grow in confidence in learning ability.

"Parenting a kinesthetic child is hard work," said Gretchen. "But the rewards are fantastic." Karen became a fine student, cooperative and happy, but her mom admits there is an investment of time. She couldn't memorize the multiplication tables by just sitting down and reading silently over them or saying them to herself. "It takes more time to be involved than to say 'Learn your multiplication tables yourself,'" said her mom.

She mastered addition and subtraction by counting rocks and little blocks, and the rougher the texture of an object, the more it held her attention. Karen learned the multiplication tables better by walking around the house reciting and being quizzed with flash cards while riding in the car. She has a marvelous attention span for things she can be actively involved with.

LEARNING TO THINK VISUALLY

Even kinesthetic students who don't naturally perceive things visually can improve their visual memory and thinking skills. Tom Cruise, the actor, faced dyslexia and accompanying reading problems in his growing-up years in school. Always in remedial classes—in fifteen different schools, because of moving—his problems worsened.

His mother, who had special-ed training, recognized his need and helped him overcome his learning problems. The number-one strategy was learning to focus his attention and learning to think visually. "I became very visual," Cruise said, "and learned to create mental images in order to comprehend what I read."[6] He also learned he had to work harder than everyone else to make it. By extra effort and improving his visual skills, he brought his reading up to grade level by his junior year of high school. Try some of the activities for improving visual skills in the chapters on auditory learning and visual learning.

Visual cues will help the kinesthetic learner. Post a picture of what your child's room looks like when it is clean on your child's bulletin board or door and it will give him or her a pattern when it's time to sort through the rubble. Tape a picture of a place setting with fork, spoon, knife, etc., inside a cupboard door to aid setting the table properly.

STRATEGIES TO ENHANCE KINESTHETIC AND TACTILE LEARNING

Reading
Perhaps the most important task of every child is to learn to read effectively, to build reading comprehension and speed. Almost 90 percent of all school learning requires reading. After third grade all subjects are dependent on reading. Don't let your child fall into being

the poorest reader or being placed in the lowest reading group. *Do not* accept a "reading disabled" label! Find a method that builds on your child's strengths and meets his or her needs. Teach your child to read at home yourself, or get a good tutor. "If kids can't learn the way we teach, we need to teach them the way they learn," says Terri Cooter, a special-education teacher and psychometrician. "If you can identify that one area of strength, you can build on it, they can learn to be good readers, and they can compensate."

If that strength is kinesthetic, visual phonics or alphabetic phonics might be best. Visual phonics gives students all the areas they can draw from—especially the kinesthetic and visual—and strengthens their auditory processing. Alphabetic phonics is a multisensory method that involves hearing, seeing, and writing the letters and words in the air. It's important to identify children's strengths early so they don't get into a pattern of failure. And you can supplement with a multisensory reading method at home even if your child is not progressing with the reading program at school. There are *many* excellent learn-to-read programs, and one will be right for your child. Chapter 8, "How Learning Styles Impact Reading Skills," will chart some of the most commonly used reading methods and the modalities they address. It will also offer some creative multisensory approaches to helping your kinesthetically strong child learn to read and to boosting his or her interest in reading.

A Large Chalkboard

A large chalkboard or white (dry-erase) chalkless board in your child's room is a great resource for a kinesthetic learner. On it your child can practice larger movements in writing spelling words or answers being studied for a test. Sliding closet doors can even be painted with chalkboard paint. If you have a dry-erase white board, different colors of markers can be used, or if a black or green board, colored chalk.

Let your child write the words in the air and then on the chalkboard as he or she says each letter in the word, and then the whole word. Your child can trace the letters with two fingers until the word is erased. Then have your child close his or her eyes and try to "see" or picture the word spelled correctly in his or her mind's eye. Then, the night before the test, a parent can call out each word while the child writes it on the board for a practice test.

The large chalkboard can also be used to work math problems, outline a chapter in any subject, or draw a large mind map. And best of all, the child can use it when he or she "teaches" the material to the family the night before a test. In this active way of studying, the child can internalize the concepts as he or she explains them to someone else. *Research shows that learners who teach information to other people retain 90 percent of it.*[7] The child may even discover he or she enjoys teaching! Kinesthetic learners can make *the* most dynamic, effective teachers.

Math for Movers and Touchers

Kinesthetic learners who are pushed too early into abstract math concepts and symbols, made to memorize by rote and apply concepts they don't understand often develop "math phobia." Although they may have a lot of potential to be excellent math students, they are being taught backwards. Math should be taught—especially to these kids—*from the concrete to the abstract*. Let him pour a half gallon of water into quart jars and pint measuring bottles to see how much the jars and bottles equal. Let her measure the walls of her bedroom with a yardstick, a twelve-inch ruler, and a long metal measuring tape to see how many inches equals a yard and how many feet are in the perimeter of her whole room. The more your mover can experience hands-on math, the more concepts he or she can understand and master.

And the more you can build solid foundations incorporating math into everyday life *before* your child starts school, the better. There are some excellent ways below. In addition to these, continue to provide manipulatives at home for your child to use while calculating and doing math work sheets and story or word problems in textbooks.

■ Family chores and activities such as sorting laundry, sorting silverware, and setting the table are good practice in learning a pattern (a fundamental math skill) and categorizing. Children can count toys while putting them away in bins or shelves, count out cookies and apples, and count Volkswagen Bugs while traveling.

■ One of the most important concepts preschoolers need to learn is *what's alike and what's different, what's greater than and what's less than,* and the best way to learn it is with concrete objects and everyday things. Put several objects out in a row and ask, "Which one is different?" Fill three glasses with different amounts of water and ask, "Which one has more?" As you see things in the neighborhood and on errands, ask, "How are the things alike? How are they different? Which is biggest?"

■ When you're reading to your child, pause before the end and ask, "What will happen next?" This gives your child an opportunity to develop deductive reasoning skills, and a sense of direction in math thinking and problem solving.

■ Another vital skill is to *find the missing part.* Ask, "All of our family is not here; how many are gone?" "There were six sodas in the refrigerator; now there are only two. How many are missing?" This lays the groundwork for algebra concepts like finding the missing variable.[8]

Math Manipulatives in the Home

Provide math manipulatives at home and encourage your child to use them when doing homework. When Kathy's son Dave couldn't understand how addition and subtraction connect, she got some plastic centimeter rods of different colors, wrote the numbers on the corresponding rods, and then had him add and subtract some numbers. After only a few minutes, the light bulb went on! While manipulating the rods, he instantly understood the concept, whereas when he looked at symbols and numbers on a page in his math workbook, he couldn't get it. (To obtain math manipulatives see addresses listed in the appendix, pages 189-193.)

When seven-year-old Jannea has items to count—Lincoln logs, bingo markers, buttons—she does much better in math. Little red balls that fit on pegs for a bingo game helped her see and feel when she was counting by fives. One mom used peanut butter sandwiches to teach the distributive properties of multiplication.

$$3(A + B) = 3A + 3B$$

Peanut Butter (White Bread + Dark Bread)

$$P(W + D) = PW + PD$$

Manipulatives are not childish, however, and can be used with any age student. High school science and math teachers of physics, chemistry, calculus, and geometry have found that their students, no matter how bright, found manipulatives challenging to make and motivating to use.

For early computation skills, you can also buy or make a big stack of number cards, including five zeros, five ones, five twos, and so forth up to ten. Then you can make up games that offer practice in calculating. You pick a card (four) and your child picks a card (six) and you each count out the right number of buttons (or bingo counters or other colored objects) for your card. Then see who has more and who has less.

Hang up a string across the room and let your child clothespin numbers up in order. Clip two numbers up—twenty-five on one side and forty on the other. Then call out a number (thirty-seven) and have your child clip it up where it goes. Continue in this fashion until all the numbers are in order. Ordering numbers and putting a value to them is an important skill.

Once your creativity gets going, the sky's the limit on all the ways you can help your child get hands-on practice in math. At the grocery store, your child can practice estimating your bill, redeeming coupons, and weighing produce on the big scales. You can call attention to batting averages and other sports statistics in the newspaper for your athletically minded child. Lemonade stands and money-making businesses are great ways for kids to learn about money and profits.

More T/K Learning Strategies

Here are some more strategies to help your tactile-kinesthetic child learn:

- Spelling snakes—Print spelling words on a laminated piece of construction paper. Roll out "snakes" or long pieces of clay. The student puts clay over the letters so that the spelling words are written with clay.
- Cookie-sheet words—Write spelling words with play dough or shaving cream on a cookie sheet.
- Globe find—Your child and a friend each have a globe. Call out a country, ocean, continent, etc., and say "Go." The one who runs across the room and places his or her finger on the correct spot on the globe first wins that round. You can also drill your child individually.
- Map find—With a U.S. map, call out a capital, abbreviation, motto, or state nickname and say "Go." Your child runs over to the map and touches the correct state to gain a point.
- Magna doodle—A portable magnetic drawing/writing board is great for the T/K learner to write spelling words or practice working math problems, etc. (good in car, desk, or small space).
- Rap song or cheer—Make up a rap song or cheer with spelling or vocabulary words.
- Puzzles—These are great for learning the fifty states and the continents.
- Sign language—"My daughter in elementary school had a hard time with spelling," said one mother. "She tried writing the words and saying them aloud, but couldn't remember. Then she taught herself sign language in the fourth grade, and from then on when she studied, she spelled them aloud while spelling in sign language. She immediately learned the words!" The "Visual Phonics" method of learning to read uses a form of sign language. (See appendix, page 193.)
- Simon Says—This game is good practice in following directions while integrating movement and play. The person being Simon says to the players, "Simon says pat your head while jumping up and down four times." Players do

the actions *only* if the leader says "Simon says" before the instruction.

Games to Build Skills

Educators are finding that children lack the skills they used to acquire from playing games and cards at home. Many of these games helped children learn math concepts such as counting, visual discrimination, and problem solving while still being active, interacting with friends, and having fun. Active, hands-on learners are engaged by these activities because with them they can learn through concrete experiences and manipulate materials (as in dice for a multiplication activity). Board games such as Chutes and Ladders, checkers, Go to the Head of the Class, and Monopoly offer a myriad of opportunities for the development of verbal skills, math skills, and thinking skills they will need to handle many intellectual tasks. A deck of playing cards is one of the least expensive and best "educational toys" there is, says Dr. Margie Golick, senior psychologist at the Learning Centre of McGill Montreal's Children's Hospital. The card game of hearts, for example, provides practice in categorizing, counting, judging quantitative rank of numbers, maintaining a variable set, adding (including adding negative numbers), reasoning, memory, calculating probabilities, and developing strategies. Even an easy game like Go Fish helps young children learn number names and practice matching and visual discrimination skills, left-right concepts, and taking turns.[9] And playing a game can be a valuable time of interaction for you and your child.

Making a Game to Study for a Test

Making a game with material to be studied involves creativity and higher-order thinking skills. It also is a great way to reinforce vocabulary, organize information, and increase comprehension of the material—in any subject. The game can be as simple as a crossword puzzle or word bingo or a board game with a spinner.

First the student gathers together the textbook, class notes, old quizzes, study cards, and any handouts on the material to be studied. Cardboard, poster board, or even a manila file folder can be used for the playing board. The board can be laminated. The path of spaces can be made with ruler and felt-tip markers. Dice, spinner, and pieces to move around the board, if it is a board game, are essential; glue, tape, ruler, and other materials will also be helpful in making the game. The child does the artwork (it could be a cooperative or group venture). Then there needs to be someone to play the game with— a classmate, brother, sister, or parent.

Make a Practice Test

Another active study method kinesthetic learners benefit from is to make a practice test with the material assigned—much more effective than falling asleep reading the information over and over! The student writes out a variety of sample questions from the class notes and textbook, such as true-false, multiple-choice, matching, and fill-in-the-blank. If the teacher includes essay questions, the student should include a few.

A friend in the class makes out a different practice test. The next day after school, the two exchange tests, score them, and see which areas they need to study more. The practice test can be done on paper or on computer. Some students get so good at making practice tests that they are able to guess many of the questions the teacher prepares for the real test and thus "ace" it!

Organizational Skills for T/K Learners

Organizational skills are important for all students, but active learners, who usually tend to be scattered with their papers and books, need them most of all. At the secondary level the number-one reason for failure is disorganization. Jackie Kelly, a special education teacher and private tutor, said that recently a tenth-grade girl was referred to her for evaluation and tutoring, because the school suspected she was "learning disabled." Upon testing her, Jackie found she had no diagnosable disability. But she was so scattered and disorganized—class notes all over the place, a textbook lost—she couldn't even pull together her materials to study for a test. No wonder she was failing. Once she got an organizational system that worked for her, her grades came up.

Here are some organizational tips for T/K learners:

- Especially for younger children, allow a break and time to play after school before homework is started.
- Provide a consistent time and place to do homework. Any quiet place away from the distraction of television is fine— a kitchen table or even on a bed with a lap-desk, if that is your child's preference.
- Assist your child in organizing his or her desk or study zone and keeping it free from distracting things that aren't related to the tasks at hand.
- Help divide homework into short study sections. Time the sessions, and after twenty minutes (or task completed) have a short break for a cookie or to play with the dog for five minutes, then finish homework.
- Have an assignment notebook or calendar with the daily schedule as visible as possible throughout the school day. For some students, it is best to *tape* the schedule on the outside cover of the main notebook that goes to each class. Then, when each teacher gives the assignment, your child can write it down.
- Be a homework consultant and supporter—brainstorm for story ideas your child can write, together read aloud a history chapter, etc.—but don't do the assignment for your child. The goal is to help the child find and use organizational and study methods that maximize his strengths and manage his weaknesses. This is important through the elementary and middle school years, so that by the time he is in ninth grade, he has become more and more independent with homework.
- Supply your child with a homework backpack—one pouch for teacher notes and completed homework and one pouch for books and notebook—and have a specific place by the door to put "school stuff" for the next day.

For many more organizational suggestions see my book *Helping Your Child Succeed in Public School* (Focus on the Family, 1993).

Adapt a Visual or Auditory Study Method to the Student's Needs
The student who needs movement can make audiotapes of the notes
or questions and answers to be studied and then listen to them on
a Walkman. That way, the student can hear and verbally practice the
information while walking, running, or jumping.

Taking good notes in class and from reading is important for
this student, but mapping or clustering the information appeals
more to the kinesthetic learner than a linear I.A.1.a. outline. That
way, the student makes a visual representation of the concepts and
facts, and knows how to connect the ideas together. Combine that
with the student explaining it verbally to you, and/or putting it on
the large chalkboard, and you have great reinforcement! (See chapter 7 for how the cluster outline would look.)

If you have a stationary bike, your child could ride it while reading a book propped up on a handlebar stand. Teachers who have let
reluctant readers try biking and reading simultaneously find it
increased their speed and comprehension. Geography facts or history questions can be called out and answered while your child jumps
on a rebounder or shoots Nerf balls in the basket.

Since you can't always use an active approach for all classroom
assignments, it's important to develop and use your child's secondary
strength. If that is visual, try some visual study strategies. If it is
auditory, develop and enhance that modality.

ENCOURAGING PRESCHOOLERS' KINESTHETIC SKILLS

▶ Preschoolers need resources for developing physical coordination, such as playground equipment, a balance beam (which you
can make out of cement blocks and a sturdy board), balls of all sizes,
riding toys, beanbag tosses, etc. In addition, they need chances to
skip, hop, jump rope, catch and throw a ball. Some of the best opportunities for parents to talk and listen to "mover" children of any age
come when they're actively engaged with you, such as when throwing a baseball or football together.

▶ Learn colors and counting skills and increase observation skills
by taking special theme walks. One day it could be a "smelly walk"

where you observe and identify smells along the way. Another day, a "color walk" to look for all the blue things in your path. Another day, counting houses or dogs on your walk around the block.

▶ Increase your child's concentration and on-task focus by regularly working togehter on a mini-project from start to finish. Just fifteen or twenty minutes of doing and focusing on *one thing*—putting together a puzzle, finger painting a picture, or making a simple craft—will help develop the ability to focus in the classroom, crucial to school success.

▶ Let your preschooler cook with you in the kitchen and learn to follow a simple recipe (there are many great microwave and other cookbooks for kids). In doing so, he or she learns about measuring, temperature, time, and other reading-readiness and math concepts.

▶ Provide a lot of hugs, pats, and physical affection. "Mover" kids have a greater need for physical affirmation that doesn't go away as they grow. Joy, a mother of two, talked to me in a personal interview about the importance of physical touch for her young daughter.

> My six-year-old daughter has a definite need for physical contact when tackling difficult work. She hangs on me, gets into my lap, tries to sit on my chair. I have spent much time and energy shooing her off me, and explaining my need for some personal space. Result: frustration on her part, guilt on my part.
>
> Now I'm seeing this need as part of her learning style, and am accommodating it. At certain times, I ask her to stand beside my chair at the table while I put my arm around her. This really seems to infuse her with courage to deal with the new information she's tackling on her home-school work. Sometimes I place my chair very close to her desk and lean toward her. This proximity seems to provide reassurance. I've put two and two together. My daughter may simply be trying to reestablish a degree of closeness that was abruptly interrupted during my difficult pregnancy and the first two years of our caring for our son with cerebral palsy. In any case, the physical touch is helping her now.

Sometimes just a touch or pat on the shoulder can help a child refocus on his or her tasks in the classroom. And one of the great rewards of being with this child is the hugs and warmth he or she gives in return!

As you adapt hands-on study methods like those in this chapter to your child's active learning style, you'll find your child will become more aware of how he or she learns and remembers best. In the next chapter, we will look at visual learning and ways to enhance visual skills in your child.

CHAPTER SEVEN

WATCHERS
VISUAL LEARNING

Holly noticed her mom's new dress before anyone else in the family. From an early age she told stories that were rich in pictorial imagery and description. When her parents would ask her how she thought up the story, she said, "It's just the movie going on in my mind!" Because of her fine visual skills, Holly was an excellent student in most subjects, especially spelling. After looking at a list of twenty words a few times, she could spell them almost perfectly. "Spelling was so easy because I could read the words off a screen in my mind just like someone was holding it up. It's not like I had to work at thinking how the word sounded."

Chris, our middle son, was entertained by his surroundings, by seeing people, by his fascination with colors and shapes of things as a baby. He didn't need action going on all the time to be happy. He could beat me anytime on word finds and big multipiece puzzles. When his dad showed him how to tie a bow tie at a young age, he learned quickly. He was exceptionally observant, had a great imagination, and loved dressing up in a costume he made and pretending he was a firefighter, Corporal Rusty, or an Indian chief.

As an honor high school student with an excellent visual memory, Chris received only one criticism from his teachers: He was "too quiet" in class (some teachers would give anything for a class of quiet kids!). They often said he didn't ask enough questions or participate enough in discussions. An independent student, he said some of his favorite times of learning came from reading the *World Book Encyclopedia* from volumes A to Z. By age eight, he had read almost every volume, on a myriad of subjects he was curious about. Actually, he would rather learn about something by reading about it than sitting and listening to someone talk on and on in a lecture.

From the many pictures he drew in childhood to the four years of art he took in high school, creating sculptures, watercolors, and portraits has remained one of his favorite pastimes.

"If I have a list of German vocabulary words to memorize for an exam," said Tiffany, a visually oriented college student, "I study the list, study my notes, and then if I think or hear the German words, I see the English equivalent as if written on a piece of paper." For oral exams, if she rereads the German stories and conversations, she is able to repeat almost the exact text because she remembers what it looked like on the page. Tiffany has a better visual memory for words than numbers or pictures. She is not art-oriented, and her second strongest modality is auditory—her favorite subjects being German, Spanish, public speaking, and English literature.

Students like Holly, Chris, and Tiffany have visual skills that they have learned to use in the classroom. Some visual students remember words best (like Tiffany), some recall pictures best, some call up numbers best, and some all three—words, pictures, and numbers. When you try to read them something, this type of learner says, "Let me see it on the page." When you tell them how to do something, they say, "Show me and I'll do it!" They like to *see* what they are learning. They like quiet surroundings for their study sessions, and need to work at uncluttered desks to concentrate the best. They also benefit from illustrations, diagrams, and charts, and often make their own pictorial representations of the concepts when taking notes.

HELPING STUDENTS HARNESS VISUAL STRENGTHS

Some students have good visual abilities but haven't learned to use them in academics. Judy was a creative artist, could recreate a still-life drawing from figures on the table in art class, and could make pictures in her mind easily when reading her favorite ski or fitness magazines, but when it came to transferring these visual abilities to the mounds of reading she had to do for history, English, and life science, she drew a blank. Many students like Judy can harness these skills in visual learning to maximize their study time and achieve more at school. Many ways to do this are given below.

Jared loves pictures, baseball cards, drawing, and fixing things. He can see a picture or diagram and put together whatever the directions show. In the car he sees landmarks and details and asks, "Dad, did you see that sign?" However, Jared had a tendency to really procrastinate in his schoolwork. He'd dawdle and doodle around with a ten-minute task for thirty or forty-five minutes. When his mom, Sherry, began to capitalize on visual abilities, he got a lot more done. She now writes all of his assignments down with a time limit and gives him a kitchen timer. "This spelling list will take you fifteen minutes. This math sheet will take you approximately thirty minutes."

To help him stay organized, Jared's mom uses a different color paper for each subject's work—history, green; language arts, yellow; etc.—and color-codes it to a matching folder. He makes illustrated time lines in history and posters and models of concepts in science. She uses yellow sticky notes to remind him of chores he needs to do around the house. With the new ways of working, he's getting twice as much done.

VISUAL LEARNERS IN THE CLASSROOM

Some of a visually strong student's skills are a great benefit in the classroom. A student with visual strengths remembers approximately 70 to 75 percent of what she sees or reads the first time. The visual student:

- Has a good sight vocabulary; uses picture clues in reading.
- Keeps an organized desk and remembers where to put things back.
- Scores well on standardized, multiple-choice, and matching tests.
- Usually becomes a rapid reader and has good comprehension.
- Can follow directions on work sheets, diagrams, and written-down instructions.
- Often excels in map skills and math computation.
- Likes to work puzzles, word finds, and visual games.
- Prefers art class to music class.[1]

However, in the classroom, visual learners often get frustrated with oral drill. Josh's third-grade math teacher started the "Twenty Second Club," in which students became official members if they could say the multiplication families in twenty seconds. The children practiced at home and said them in front of the class while the teacher checked off the family groups. When all students reached the twelve family, she was going to throw a pizza party. This was a wonderful activity for the auditory learners! They loved it and were the first to make the "Twenty Second Club." But Josh still hadn't made the club after his third week of trying.

Visual learners should realize that while they learn fast, they can forget equally fast. Think of the mind like a Polaroid camera. The picture develops quickly, but unless emulsion is used on the picture to stabilize it, the images can fade rapidly. In the learning process, the "emulsion" is to write as well as look at the information.

Visual learners can also have trouble with oral directions and may ask, "What are we supposed to do now?" right after the teacher has explained it. When this irritates the teacher or she says, "You weren't listening," anxiety in the student can build. The fact is, the student probably was listening, but needs a visual or graphic representation of what the directions are—on the board or on a sheet on the desk—to do his or her best. Learning to read with an entirely phonetic-based approach proved frustrating and difficult for Josh.

(Check chapter 8 for the best methods for visual students.) And unless he and other visual learners become really good note takers, they will tend to tune out class lectures and presentations.

In addition to the strategies below, chapter 11, "Your Child in the Classroom," will give many tips on working with visual learners in the school situation, communicating with the teacher, and providing compensating strategies.

Make sure your child has an eye exam by the age of three, because vision problems can cause learning problems in children. Nearsightedness; farsightedness; crossed eyes; and lazy eye, or amblyopia—the main reasons kids need glasses—can all affect reading ability and the ability to see the symbols and letters on the board. In first through third grade, 10 to 15 percent of children wear glasses, and in later grades, 20 percent. Most vision problems can be corrected and the child's learning not be adversely affected.

VISUAL LEARNING

Any time visual students can change or translate a chapter into a diagram, chart, or drawing, it will help them understand and retain what they read. Here are some ways to help visual learners capitalize on their strengths.

Outline and Graphically Represent Ideas

All students need to develop good note-taking skills for classroom lectures and orally presented material. This is especially important for visual learners because just listening to someone talk tends to put them to sleep and brings on a major attack of boredom. To keep tuned in and learning, visual learners must record and remember information. Here are some good ways to do that:

Index cards. You can use three-by-five-inch or four-by-six-inch index cards in any subject. For example, in geography: Write the state on front and the capital on back (include a drawing if desired). In French or other foreign language: French word on front, English equivalent on back. In history, science, or literature: question on front, answer on back.

Index cards can also be used for a variety of purposes—note taking in class, textbook highlights, or for vocabulary and key words to learn for a test. They are handy because you can slip them in your pocket and bring them out several times a day to read and review while waiting in line or if extra minutes remain in class. You can use the study cards to make a tape recording to listen to and review.

Early elementary students can write each letter of the alphabet on index cards and draw an accompanying picture with felt-tip, colored pens. They can also write difficult words from the day's reading assignment on one side of the cards and illustrate them on the other side. After the words are written and illustrated, someone can go over them with the student orally (either at school or at home); if the student forgets a word, the student can refresh his or her memory by looking at the illustration on the flip side. That way, the student develops a mental picture for each word.

Index cards can slide into your child's pocket. They can also fit in a zip-lock bag and go in a backpack or anywhere the child goes— perfect for "studying on the go." In addition, absorbing the amount of information on an index card is quicker and less overwhelming than studying everything on an eight-by-eleven-inch sheet of paper.[2] If your child likes color, you can get a different color of card for each class. A file box is an efficient way to store the study cards to prepare for the six-week, nine-week, or semester test.

Mind maps. Also called semantic or learning maps, these pictorial representations of information are great ways to organize, learn, and remember, both in and out of the classroom. They are similar to the "clustering" pre-writing activity shown in chapter 5. Since the mind map uses visual and verbal skills, and thus both sides of the brain, it boosts learning and memory. Constructing the map helps the student see and understand the connection between key ideas, and increases comprehension of the material. Organized information is much easier to remember and retrieve at test time or a later date. Mind maps can be written on paper or on four-by-six-inch index cards.

The main topic or concept goes in the middle, and the related ideas on lines leading to the subtopics. On page 105 there is a representation of a visual map of the Battle of Gettysburg and the who,

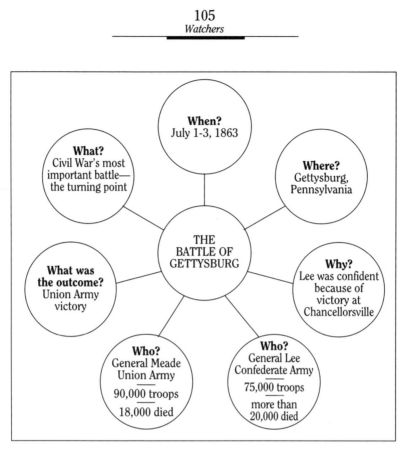

what, when, where, and how information that I jotted down after reading about it in the encyclopedia and seeing the movie *Gettysburg*.

The visual student usually enjoys outlining the material in this way; it provides a visual cue to recall during study and test times, which is much better than several pages of expository information. After the student makes the map, he or she should discuss the information pictured with someone else—a study partner, small group, or you. The student should review it each day leading up to the test. Then, the day before the exam, he or she should try to write it on his white chalkless board or blackboard, explaining it to someone else. When taking notes, any way the student can harness his or her natural ability to "doodle" and draw in the margins to help him or her learn and remember information, even drawing a stick figure to represent a character in history, is a boost to memory.

Illustrated time line. For history, an illustrated time line is a good way to visually depict dates, events, and key ideas of a historical period. On a large sheet of paper or even larger sheet of butcher paper, have your child write the date, the name of the event, and under it, an illustration, symbol, or cartoon that represents it. Here's an example:

Confederate Troops Attack Fort Sumter	Battle of Bull Run Confederate Victory	Lincoln Issues Emancipation Proclamation	Battle of Gettysburg Tide to Union	Confederacy Surrendered
1861	1862	1863	1863	1865

Class notes. Class notes can be recorded in a spiral notebook in this way: Have your child draw a straight line down the entire page to section off the right two-thirds. In the right section go notes from the board or teacher's lecture during class time. Then every night in the left or "recall" section, the student reads over that day's class notes, summarizes the main concepts, and writes key words and ideas. Your child can also draw a symbol or picture in the left summary section to help him or her remember the main ideas for review (more constructive doodling). On the left side of the notebook, he can write down a question that the teacher could ask on the material. The sheet would look like this:[3]

SUMMARY NOTES	CLASS NOTES
Key Words Summary Symbol or Picture of Main Ideas	Notes from board or lecture go here Question/Answer

To study, the student covers the right side, looks at the key words or symbols on the left, and sees what he or she can recall. This note-taking process helps the student integrate the concepts and connect ideas. Explaining the notes to someone is extra reinforcement.

Colored sticky notes. These are a student's tools for keeping up with tasks and questions. The student should keep a supply handy in his or her main notebook or backpack, and pull one out in each class the teacher makes an assignment. If she assigns page 25, even-numbered problems 1-30, the student should put a sticky note on page 25 with the page numbers and instructions briefly written. The note must stick out a little so when the student opens his or her locker to go home, he or she sees that the book needs to be taken home for an assignment.

Karen DeClouet, M.S., a speech/language pathologist, advises students to do the following:

- Keep at least ten blank notes adhered to the inside of every textbook, notebook, and assignment planner. "If, in the middle of a class lecture the student finds his mind wandering (and if they're honest, most students easily admit to this)," says Karen, "he should simply write that distracting thought on the sticky note and place it in his assignment planner."[4] Once the note is written, the student knows that he or she will be able to tend to the idea later and can go back to concentrating on the lesson.
- Notes inside textbooks or spiral notebooks can indicate a question the student needs to ask the teacher, or a concept the student doesn't understand.
- The sticky notes are good places to list things to do, and when stuck on the assignment notebook or desk, help the student get and stay organized.

Limit Television Viewing

Visual kids tend to watch more television than auditory or kinesthetic kids because they love the visual stimulation. As one mom I know said, "My auditory daughter Lauren watches a minimum of television because she'd rather be talking on the telephone, listening to music, or being with friends. My kinesthetic son is too busy riding his bike, jumping on the trampoline, or occupied with a project in the garage. But Jared, my little visual guy, will stare at the tube for hours! I can hardly get him away from it unless it's to play a video game."

If your child is like Jared, limit television viewing. When he or she does watch, sit down together to watch and then *talk about the program*. Your child needs to be reading, pursuing hobbies, studying, and doing other activities. The highest achieving high school students in North America spend an average of seventeen hours a week studying and only about four hours a week watching television. But most teens spend five and a half hours on homework and twenty-one to twenty-three hours watching television. Preschoolers should watch no more than thirty minutes to an hour a day.

Highlighting

Another way for visual students to focus on their strengths is highlighting important information that needs to be learned. Highlighting is also helpful to kinesthetic students, because they're writing and busy with their hands. Often students will buy a colored highlighter and proceed to highlight everything on the page, which doesn't turn out to be very helpful in remembering key words or concepts. Instead, students should buy a variety of colored highlighters: pink, blue, yellow, orange, green. Then they can color-code information. For a history chapter, for example, key concepts are highlighted in yellow, answers to key chapter questions in pink, vocabulary words in green, and definitions in orange. In English, to facilitate identifying the parts of speech: green for nouns, blue for verbs, yellow for modifiers (adjectives and adverbs), and pink for connectives. In science, highlighting aids classification, vocabulary, and reading comprehension. And in math, the student can highlight the main points in word problems and the answer in another color.

Highlighting helps integrate the right- and left-hemisphere thinking skills because the color and patterns of coding appeal to the right (global) and the words and numbers to the left (analytic). Encourage your child, regardless of learning style, to try highlighting with color, and see it help your child be more active and able to absorb more when reading. By using the color-coded material to study with, your child will have better retrieval of the information for tests.

Computers

"My son learns best by putting spelling words or notes from science on his computer," said one mother. She calls out his spelling words orally and he types them into the computer. "He then is able to see the information and concentrate on studying it." They have found he retains the information much better than when he reads or studies from a book.

Computers offer many possibilities for all learning styles, and visual students especially enjoy the stimulation. Composing and editing on a word-processing program facilitate writing skills. Drill and practice in math, spelling, vocabulary, and other subjects can be done with computer games and activities. Children's books are being put into electronic form to be "read" on personal computers, with the added appeal of animated illustrations and sound effects. Although these should never replace reading printed books to and with your child, they can be a creative addition to learning.

There is a world of excellent educational software for home use. Ask the school's computer lab coordinator or your child's classroom teacher to recommend the best software with educational, not just entertainment, benefits.

Writing Assignments

One of the best strategies to facilitate students' writing is *mapping the story*. I have used this pre-writing activity with young authors from first grade to college, with great results. It's not a new idea: Robert Louis Stevenson drew a watercolor map of an island to entertain his stepson on a rainy London day, and that map grew into his famous classic, *Treasure Island.*

First, I draw a rough sketch or "map" of my own grade school on the chalkboard—or better, with bright markers on a large sheet of butcher paper taped up—and begin to relate the story of how I was injured and got my first stitches out on the asphalt playground, then my first black eye on the softball field, and after that got into a bunch of trouble on the high jungle gym. Each place where an incident happened, I put an *X*.

Then I have the students make a map of a place they remember:

summer camp, Grandma's farm, the first house they remember living in. If it's a house, they draw the outline of the rooms (but not the furniture and detail—this is only a rough sketch. Students who are detail-oriented can add more later, even color if they desire). Then they put an *X* wherever an incident occurs to them. After completing their map, they rehearse the story orally by telling it to a partner.

After approximately ten minutes of storytelling (five for each person), the students begin to write the story on paper. Some of the most wonderful stories—by all kinds of learners of all ability levels—are written because they have "seen" the story, "talked and heard" the story, and the ideas and sequence of events flow rapidly! These are later illustrated, edited, and published in a class anthology; posted on the walls of the hall or bulletin board; or sometimes even made into a collection of personal-experience stories in a book. This pre-writing mapping activity can be done just as well at home to generate writing for a school assignment.

A picture is another good way to stimulate the visual student's writing. Give the student a selection of a few interesting pictures with characters and some action going on, or just a fascinating scene. Have the student choose one of the pictures and write a story about it.

Here's another visual story-writing springboard: Give the student a long piece of paper and ask him or her to fold it into fours. Then the student draws an illustration for the beginning of the story, two for the middle, and one for the end, and then shares the story orally with another person before writing it down.

Geography Memory Booster
Put a big, colorful map of the United States or world on the bedroom wall, close to your child's desk, or in the family room near the television set. When news reports highlight a city, state, or country, have your child note it on the map and put a small colored circle on it (which you can get at office-supply stores). Just seeing the map on a regular basis helps the student get an internal picture of the location of cities, states, rivers, mountain ranges, etc.

Illustrating Math Problems

Visually representing story problems with real-life objects—pictures the student, parent, or teacher draws—helps in comprehension and problem solving. Story problems can also be illustrated with magazine pictures by pasting a picture to a card containing the applicable story problem. In pairs, the children can figure out how to work the problem, and then they pass the picture on to the next pair to work.

When the teacher describes a triangle or rectangle and its characteristics, the visual student should try to picture the shape in his or her mind. When the student can visualize the problem by making pictures or tallies of it on scratch paper as it is discussed, the student will be able to work it more quickly and correctly.

Writing Down Chores

If chores at home and assignments at school are *written down*, children will do a 100-percent better job of following through and getting them done. Karen found this out by working with her ten-year-old son, Jacob. When she asked him orally to go get her school briefcase and turn off the computer (while she was tutoring a student), he forgot one or both instructions. But when later she handed him a yellow note with the two requests, he quickly went in, got her bag, turned off the computer, and delivered it, saying, "Anything else, Mom?" Often what we think is misbehavior is just misdirection. If you will write down the instructions, and have your child cross them off as he or she completes them, you'll be amazed at the cooperation!

ENHANCING LOW VISUAL SKILLS

If your child is weak in visual learning, or is a preschooler or elementary student, and you want to enhance visual skills that will add to his or her readiness for school learning, try these activities:

Memory tray. While your child is watching, place five objects on a tray one at a time, such as a comb, dollar bill, spoon, toy car, and pencil. Have your child look at them closely for forty-five seconds. Then take the tray away and have your child close his eyes and see if he can "see" the objects and name them. Can he name the objects in the order they were placed on the tray? Can he name them in reverse order? Then put three of the same objects and one or two new ones on the tray and repeat the game. This is a good way to develop visual memory and recall.

Seeing and describing. Have your child look at something: an interesting picture; an object such as a bouquet of flowers or a toy you place on the table in front of her; or something you see as you are driving, like an animal or barn. Then have her close her eyes and describe it as vividly as possible; next have her open her eyes and see how well she described the object.[5]

Storytelling the visual way. Have your child choose a familiar story, read it from a book (however many times is necessary), and then practice relating it orally the way real storytellers do. Ask him to picture the story *by scenes* in his mind—that is, create a "mental movie" of the characters doing the action, scene by scene. Then have him tell the story, adding his own gestures, dialect, and even props. Have fun telling the story!

Board games. Have your child play board games, many of which develop visual discrimination skills and verbal skills at the same time (such as Chutes and Ladders). Monopoly, Scrabble for Juniors or regular Scrabble, Connect Four, Chinese checkers, and other games enable the child to have fun and yet learn and build skills at the same time. Games are a much better use of time than watching television!

Card games. Teach your child to play card games and encourage her to play cards with friends. Besides counting and sequencing, logic and strategy skills, card games as easy as Go Fish and War to more difficult games like hearts, rummy, and spades build visual discrimination skills, visual memory, visual alertness, visual tracking (the ability to move the eyes smoothly to scan any plane and spot important details), eye-hand coordination, and many other important abilities children need for success in reading and math.[6]

The card game Concentration (see directions in chapter 5) is a great game for strengthening visual memory and recall in even the poorest spellers. An excellent resource for the use of playing cards in teaching and learning is *Deal Me In!* by Dr. Margie Golick, chief psychologist at the Learning Centre of the McGill-Montreal Children's Hospital.

Transparency sheets. Students with low visual skills can be helped by allowing them to use a colored transparency sheet such as rose or teal over a page of print. It can reduce glare, which causes some students difficulty in concentrating and reading.[7] Colored transparency sheets can be purchased at teacher-resource stores or office-supply stores. Try this at home and if it helps, talk to the teacher.

Kids who discover how to best utilize their visual strengths enjoy learning more and grow in confidence. As you help enhance visual development in the ways suggested in this chapter, your child will grow to be observant and save valuable time. Improving the visual memory or "Xeroxer" in your child's brain will help him or her excel in areas of interest—whether that is art, science, or another field.

If your child has two dominant modalities, like visual/kinesthetic or visual/auditory strengths, try combining methods of study. Reinforce with a different learning strategy from the appropriate chapter, and then encourage your child to use the information in a creative, active way. In the next chapter, we'll look at how learning styles impact reading skills and how to make sure your child gets a solid foundation in reading.

CHAPTER EIGHT

HOW LEARNING STYLES IMPACT READING SKILLS

When Debra introduced the initial letter sounds to her six-year-old daughter Mary with the Spalding reading program, it just wasn't clicking. Mary was not remembering the sounds and was distracted by the things going on around her in the room. Debra felt her daughter's strengths were visual and kines-thetic, so she decided to come up with a multisensory approach to learning to read. She made a tape recording of the initial phono-grams (or sounds) that the letters made. She then wrote the phono-grams in large letters on brightly colored cards. She taped the let-ter-sound cards in order all the way around the room, gave Mary a flashlight, and turned the light out in the room.

As the tape played and Mary heard it, she spoke the letter sound, traced around the letter with her flashlight, and then went on to the next card until she had gone all the way around the room. "It kept her attention; it was fun, and reinforced the auditory, visual, and kinesthetic modalities," said her mom. On different days Mary traced the letters with glue and then sand and salt. As she mastered the initial sounds, they added new letter sounds until she had learned all seventy phonograms. With this creative method, everything clicked and Mary became an excellent reader.

Since reading is one of the most important challenges children face in the early grades, we as parents and teachers need to do everything we can to ensure their success. There is no perfectly right learn-to-read method that works for all children. Although it is vitally important that children have intensive phonics training as the first building block in the reading process, we don't have to stick with one "program" and exclude all other approaches and modalities.[1] In fact, an eclectic method that combines the best elements from several approaches may work well.

As was true for Mary, some children need extra help in the beginning stages of learning to read, such as individualizing the reading method and adding the component the child is strongest in. If the child is strong kinesthetically and tactilely, make sure that in addition to the phonics lessons, there is hands-on practice such as tracing the letters in the air with the hand and whole arm and/or tracing the letters with a finger in sand or salt. If the connections between the sounds and the letters are not clicking for the visually oriented learner, use picture cues and focus on the shape of the letters, then write the letters or touch them. The auditory learner should hear a word first, have the phonetic sound pointed out, trace or write it, and then use it in a game or experience.[2]

Extensive research has shown that if students are introduced to letters, words, and reading *through their strongest sense*, they achieve much higher reading competency. For example, in 1977, Karen Urbshot did research that showed that auditory children learn to read better with phonics than any other way, and that visual children do better with word recognition. In 1980, Marie Carbo won a national research award for the best contribution to the field of education. She taught auditory, visual, and tactile children to read according to their perceptual strengths. Carbo's results proved that each group of students achieved significantly more when taught reading through their perceptual strengths.[3]

Dr. Tim Campbell, assistant professor of education at the University of Central Oklahoma, told me in a personal interview, "Reading differences are common to all students. It may be that the reader is more visually oriented or a hands-on learner. Reading differences can become a disability if the child is not in a teaching-learning situation that is based both on his strengths and needs. Taking into account what the student *can do with his strengths and differences* can make the *difference* in reading success or failure."

Teachers and parents are key players in this discussion, Campbell adds, for knowing what a reader's strengths and needs (differences) are can be helpful in planning the best instruction. Parents can and should be actively involved with their child's reading and recognize reading differences. Parents' involvement can range from giving the teacher valuable information that can impact instruction to volunteering to help in their child's classroom and encouraging reading at home. It can also mean finding a tutor outside of school to teach the child to read if the child is experiencing difficulties. Sometimes it means home-schooling the child through the early years to ensure success in reading, writing, and the basic skills. What's important is to intervene *early* so that a pattern of success, not failure, is established.

Kathy, a Michigan mother, realized that the reading readiness of her third son, David, was just not where it should be for first grade. He also had some attention problems. In contrast to his two older brothers' skills at that stage, and because of the lack of progress in decoding words and recognizing sounds she saw in David's kindergarten work, she was concerned he would get behind and never really enjoy reading. Because of the pressure he would encounter to read without the skills and the undermining of his self-esteem that being in the slowest reading group would cause, Kathy decided to home-school David for first grade.

Besides his other instruction, every day for two or three hours he sat beside her so he could see the book while she read to him. During first semester she read aloud to him the entire *Little House on the Prairie* series, C. S. Lewis' *Chronicles of Narnia* books, and many other delightful classics.

By the beginning of February, David took off reading to himself in first-grade level books, and within a month had moved up to third- or fourth-grade level in his reading ability. The next year he entered school as a second grader who excelled and scored beyond grade level in reading.

Below is a guide to some common reading methods, the modalities they address, and practical things parents can do to foster their child's success in reading from the early-reader stage to fluency.

Don't accept a "reading disabled" label for your child. Often the problem is "teaching disabilities" instead—that is, the method the child is being taught is faulty or lacking in essential elements that build on his or her strongest modalities. About 20 to 30 percent of

---

READING METHODS[4]

Phonics
Auditory-intensive phonics focuses on learning letters, blends, and syllable sounds. It moves from letter combinations to sentences, paragraphs, stories.
Different programs include Spalding Method, Sing, Spell, Read & Write, or a combination of phonics with a multisensory approach (see below).

Orten Gillingham Alphabetic Phonics
Tactile, kinesthetic, auditory, visual.
Structured form of phonics, with a lot of tracing.
Student looks, says, and traces letters with fingers/sounds reinforced by all senses. Herman Method and Cooper Method similar. Successfully used with dyslexic students. More information is available through the Orton Dyslexia Society (see appendix, page 191, for address and phone number).

Visual Phonics
Visual, auditory, kinesthetic, tactile.
A system of forty-six hand signs and written symbols.
Each written symbol is a visual representation of the hand sign.
Can be used in conjunction with any good reading, literacy, or English as a second language program. (See appendix, page 193 for information.)

Whole Language[5]
Visual, auditory.
A literature-based reading and writing program.
Emphasis on the interrelationship of the language arts—reading, writing, and spelling.

Talking Books/Carbo Recorded Book Method
Visual, auditory.
High-interest books are recorded in sequential segments of six to
ten minutes each with much expression. Students listen to recording, following along with finger, repeating two or three times until
they can read fluently aloud. Books for the Blind also are an excellent resource for students who have reading problems. A student
will qualify for them if reading level is a certain number of points
below his or her intelligence.

Direct Access
Student moves from concept to picture to word to sound; used
for students who have both phonetic and semantic reading difficulties.

Look-Say, Sight Word
Visual
A rote word-memory system based on visual cues (mastering
words by examining the nearby picture and sight-word recognition
[words that appear over and over in text]).

---

children in schools have some kind of reading difficulty, but only
2 percent of the population are truly dyslexic. Letter and word rever-
sal is quite common with first and second graders but persists only
with dyslexic children.[6] Even if your child has some initial difficulties,
don't allow him or her to be labeled and put in the slowest reading
group. Have the child's reading skills evaluated by a professional,
start a home reading program that includes phonics and builds on
your child's strengths (see appendix for suggestions), get him or her
an excellent tutor, and follow the suggestions below, *but make sure
your child learns to read well.*

BOOSTING READING SKILLS, INTEREST,
AND COMPREHENSION

*Early readers need to know certain basic things about books,
letters, and words.* When you have read-aloud time, give your child
a book, point out the answers to the following questions, then go
back and ask the child:

- Where is the front, back, left, and right of each page?
- Where is the beginning of the story, the middle of the story, the end of the story?
- Where is the top of the page, the bottom of the page?
- Give your child a pencil and ask him or her to circle one word, circle one letter, circle two letters, etc.

Help your young child understand the reading-writing connection. Do this by reading aloud while the child is sitting next to you and able to see the print and pictures, and also by writing down a story as your child tells it or dictates it to you. Read your child's story back just as he or she dictated it, let the child illustrate it if he or she would like to, and staple or bind the pages together.

Read aloud at home every day. Read-aloud time should be enjoyable, relaxed, and regular. Nothing helps your child become an avid reader and develop good comprehension and language skills like being read aloud to. Even after children start school and learn to read, they need to be read to and have chances at home to read aloud to parents and siblings.

Surround your child with good books in areas of his or her interest. Building on a child's natural interests in reading is a secret to boosting his or her motivation and skills. "I was a terrible reader in elementary school," said William Jackson, one of the top marine biologists in the United States. "Until in the sixth grade, my aunt who lived in Japan sent me *The Omnibus of Science Fiction*. It was a huge volume with sixty stories about space adventures, scientists' accidents, the creation of new life forms, that ignited my imagination and stirred up my love of science." Jackson read it three or four times, and then went on to read Westerns, mysteries, and spy novels. That book opened a whole new world for him, and Jackson became a prodigious reader. He later pursued a career in marine biology and heads the National Marine Fisheries Service in Galveston, Texas.

Tap into the child's interest and you light the fire! As Karen Gale, a reading specialist who has taught hundreds of children and adults to read, says, "The first thing I do is find out what the student is interested in." Besides the combination of phonics, visual cues, cluster method, and other approaches she uses to find what the child is picking up quickest and what makes the light bulb go on (that is, makes reading happen), she asks what the child's very favorite things to learn about are. If the child is interested in topography, she uses books with pictures of volcanoes, from which the child sounds out words about volcanoes. When the student is ready, she has him or her write about volcanoes.

Provide books on tape for kids with auditory/verbal strengths or those having trouble with reading comprehension or reading speed. When they can hear and see the words, sentences, and paragraphs, silent reading comes alive.

Consider your child's learning style when picking books. Young kinesthetic learners like pop-up books, scratch-and-sniff books, and books with movable parts. Later they are drawn to adventure stories, science fiction, action stories, sports heroes' biographies, and books about certain sports. They read best when propelled by something they want to *do* (like a manual telling how to put together a go-cart). They need to see and experience books as a resource.

Auditory learners usually are book lovers, but when young they especially love rhyming nursery tales, books with poetry and rhythm or a singsong verse. They enjoy hearing you tell stories and telling stories themselves. The "listener/talker" enjoys books with developing characterization, good dialogue, and good plots.

Visual learners of all ages—even up to adults—love books with beautiful, full-color illustrations. Visual kids like wordless picture books, books like Richard Scarry's point-and-look books, books on how to draw things, and books with detailed photographs. Our son Chris often scanned through the *World Book Encyclopedia* looking for a picture that fascinated him; then he would stop to study it, and then read the accompanying article. My visual husband can spend much time looking at a pictorial Civil War history or a book of New England house designs. These picture-literate people also like books with good descriptions of the scenery and characters—it's easy for them to make a "mental movie" while reading.

Parents Sharing Books is an excellent program for parents to get involved with their elementary, middle school, or high

school child's reading. The parent gets a paperback copy of the same book the child or teen is reading, and both read it independently but share about the plot and characters, or the ideas and opinions they have on the book. In Indiana alone, over three hundred parents and kids are sharing books, growing in their communication, and boosting comprehension and motivation. (For information on Parents Sharing Books, see appendix, page 191.)

Reluctant readers and visual learners can be motivated to read if they watch a movie, such as* Black Beauty, *before reading the book. When a group of school children watched programs like "Anne of Green Gables," the movie *Raising the Titanic*, or the National Geographic specials, all the books on those subjects quickly disappeared from the school library.

If your child's reading is not progressing or is not up to grade level, locate a qualified person to evaluate your child and identify any problems in reading development. If your child is reading poorly, don't wait. Get extra help quickly! If you can work with her yourself, use phonics materials and/or mutisensory materials to help her. If you cannot work with your child, or conflict and frustration has built up due to a long-standing problem, contact a qualified reading tutor or take your child to a reputable private reading center.

As you adapt reading methods and materials to your child's learning style, read aloud as a family, and encourage daily independent reading in the child's favorite areas of interest, you will go a long way toward helping your child become a fluent, lifelong reader and a more successful student. In the next two chapters we will take a new look at what it means to be "smart" and learn how to discover and develop children's intelligence and talent.

CHAPTER NINE

ANOTHER LOOK AT SMART: PART 1
DEVELOPING YOUR CHILD'S TALENTS AND GIFTS

Each child is made by an enormously creative God. Each one is so unique! Each has a one-of-a-kind brain, special gifts and talents, and different ways of looking at life. These have a big impact not only on how the child learns but also on the child's skills and the vocation he or she chooses. Interwoven in your child's learning style—his or her way of perceiving, processing, and remembering—are the intelligence gifts and talents your child possesses. Even our memory and what we recall the best is indicative of our potential talent. The musically talented often have a fine memory for songs and musical patterns; the kinesthetically gifted dancer has a great memory for dance steps. The person with spatial talent remembers the route to a campsite better than anyone else in the hiking group, and the language-talented person remembers words the best and therefore memorizes a poem with ease. Your learning strengths are a clue to your intelligence gifts. And when a person understands his or her strengths and weaknesses, and knows and develops his or her talents, the sky's the limit on what that person can achieve.

Take Quincy Jones, for example. Creativity comes naturally to this renowned composer of the soundtracks for the movie "The Color Purple" and the miniseries "Roots" and winner of twenty-five Grammy awards. When he is composing, he sees pictures. When he sees pictures, he hears music. The ideas keep generating, and he finds himself writing in taxis or in airplanes, using menus, gum wrappers—anything that's handy—to capture ideas when the creativity is flowing. He can see and hear all the parts and pieces of a work in his head. But he admits he has limitations too, that this is all he can do. He never even learned to drive a car.

Auditory people tend to be word people; they think in words, may be creative with words, and are highly verbal. Like our son Justin, they love debates and studying in groups, and learn best by hearing explanations and practicing the information aloud. Like my friend Patsy Clairmont, a dynamic speaker, humorist, and author, they are skilled at expressing themselves. Because of their ability to process verbal information quickly and efficiently, they communicate well and tend to have good "people," or interpersonal, skills. They may become successful lawyers, writers, teachers, or radio or television broadcasters.

People with visual and spatial talent can see an object in their mind's eye and even visualize what it would look like turned around or in relation to other objects. Engineers and artists share this ability. Like my husband, Holmes, a designer and home builder, they see the painting or house before it's ever drawn or built. And like John Sabolich, the spatially talented man described in chapter 2, who loved to design spaceships as a child and now invents high-tech prostheses for amputees.

Maggie, a ballet and modern-dance teacher I know, said, "When I hear music or poetry, I think flowing shapes and see movement." Kinesthetically gifted people like Maggie learn and express themselves best through movement. They may become Olympic gold-medal winners like Greg Louganis, actors, dancers, computer experts, or sculptors.

You see, how your child learns is also a key to his or her giftedness and even purpose in life. These learning differences are not just liabilities, as we tend to think of them. So let's look at different intelligence gifts, their characteristics, and ways to develop them in our kids.

CREATIVE KIDS: PROBLEMS OR PRODIGIES?

Dean was an immensely creative child from an early age. He had a vivid, active imagination; a wonderful sense of humor; and great verbal skills. Along with the ability to be logical and conceptual, he talked with imaginary friends—like the alligator in the cold-air vent he'd feed candy wrappers to. He loved music, reading, and writing creatively. In the classroom his approach to learning was so methodical and so rapid—he'd learn the material in a few minutes—that he would then daydream, draw, or play with the kids next to him. Frequently this created some discipline problems.

"I found very few teachers who knew how to channel his boundless energy," said his mother, Sandy. Even fewer capitalized on his creativity instead of criticizing it.

In the home his parents were creative, and very encouraging to Dean. And he pursued projects and musical instruments with enthusiasm. But he began to hate school more and more. Teachers said if he would only apply himself, he'd be a top student. "We tried everything when low report cards came home—scolding, grounding. Nothing worked." The problem was, Dean didn't know how to involve his strengths in the learning process, and his talent and creativity were for the most part not appreciated or developed at school.

One insightful teacher told Dean's parents he had an enormous personality, but it would take time for him to grow into it. By eighteen or nineteen he had! Although he barely graduated from high school, he has been a mostly A college student. As a music major, he plays tuba, trombone, baritone, and guitar. He sings, composes music, and excels in any class that requires conceptual thinking and writing skills. He is a high achiever in math and in theory courses. He plans to teach music, and is married to a musician. Told by a teacher in the early grades that he needed drugs to settle down his alleged hyperactivity, he is a calm adult with tremendous energy for creating and for weekend woodworking projects, but he balances his activity with quiet, reflective times.

A SCHOOL'S EYE VIEW OF INTELLIGENCE

Society in general, and school in particular, doesn't encourage creative thinkers like Dean. Test smarts and logical-math and language abilities get kids high marks. When teachers evaluate students at the elementary level, they emphasize the social-skills aspect of their performance—behavior rather than knowledge. Students who make high grades often have excellent clerical abilities and are high in conformity. Highly creative elementary children often become school problems. At the junior high and high school level, teachers emphasize verbal skills. And at the college level, teachers emphasize problem-solving skills.[1] If your child has the "school's eye view of intelligence"—whatever that happens to be at her particular level, school, and classroom—she is affirmed by good grades and rewarded at awards assemblies. But children and teens whose strengths and talents have no place to be developed or appreciated in the school system wonder about their worth and purpose and often experience frustration in the classroom.

As Robert Sternberg, Yale professor and researcher, says, "the school's eye view of intelligence" plays "a major role in determining who succeeds and who fails, not only in school, but also in later life."[2] Students who have creative abilities or practical, real-life intelligence "may come to perceive themselves as not particularly intelligent because of their lesser test scores and the lesser reinforcement they receive in school."[3] He says they are at risk for seeing themselves as "impostors," people who succeed even though they aren't very capable or don't deserve to succeed.

Although IQ, or intelligence, tests and standardized, pencil-and-paper tests are poor measuring devices of real intelligence and talent, most schools use them to identify intellectual talent. Sternberg himself did terribly on IQ tests in elementary school. "In elementary school I had severe test anxiety," he says. "I'd hear other people starting to turn the page, and I'd still be on the second item. I'd utterly freeze." In sixth grade he did so poorly on an IQ test that he was sent to retake it with the fifth graders. But by seventh grade he was designing and administering his own test of mental ability as part of an original science project. In tenth grade he studied how distractions affect people taking mental-ability tests. Today he teaches at Yale University, has written hundreds of articles and several books on intelligence, and has received numerous fellowships and awards for his research and his "Triarchic Theory" of intelligence.[4]

Sternberg's three-sided view of intelligence, discussed later in this chapter, offers great insights for realizing your children's strengths and capitalizing on their talents.

DISCOVERING YOUR CHILD'S TALENTS

It's up to us as parents to work with our children's intelligence gifts, talents, and skills. We must

- *Recognize*
- *Develop*
- *Appreciate*

We can't depend on school to discover and nurture these abilities, although it is a real boost to our children's development when the school setting offers a place for them to use or practice their talents—such as an art class for the visually/spatially talented youngster, a music class for the budding musician, or a science fair for the scientifically curious. However, these are usually incidental, once-a-week (or once-a-year) activities—*if* the school has the money for them—rather than integral parts of the educational program.

Building on your child's strengths and discovering and nurturing his or her intelligence is a great motivation and self-esteem booster. In addition, success in one area helps children develop the momentum to work harder and succeed in tasks that are harder for them. In contrast, Dr. Mel Levine describes the "chronic success deprivation" in which a student goes through many years of life with few, if any, real triumphs and has little chance to develop his or her gifts. "A kid who is not very popular, who has school problems, and who doesn't play sports well may be deprived of success in life at that point. Sometimes a student like that just gives up or gets very depressed."[5]

It is vital to find something your child is good at and to encourage and invest in that skill! You know your child the best, care the most, and can spot talent and intelligence that school overlooks. Observing your child as your child works, plays, interacts with people, solves problems, and does homework, is one of the best ways to identify his or her strengths. All kids are born with a lot of potential in one or several areas. But research shows that the determinant factor in whether or not the young person's talent blooms is the support, encouragement, and development offered by parents.

Let's look at two perspectives of intelligence to determine your child's particular areas of strength: Sternberg's descriptions in this chapter, and Howard Gardner's model of the "multiple intelligences" in the next. Taken together, they form a broad perspective of intelligence and talent and the tools for you to find the "hidden treasure" in your child. Sternberg has identified three components of intelligence: the creative, the analytical, and the practical.

THE CREATIVE THINKER

"Academic smarts are easy to find, but creativity is rare and precious," says Sternberg.[6] He cites Barbara, a graduate student with creative thinking ability, who likes to make her own rules and be given a lot of freedom. Whether the assignment was a science project or a speech she had to give in high school, she went at the task in an innovative, fresh way. She may not make the best test scores in the class, but she has great ideas and is a very creative thinker. She is a "big picture" person who looks at the whole concept rather than the details. She has what's called "synthetic ability": the insight to combine different experiences or ideas and see them in a new way, or the ability to look at an old problem and come up with new solutions.[7]

When studying literature, for example, a student like Barbara would prefer to make up her own story with an original plot and characters rather than analyzing what various critics said about a given work. She may have scored in the average range in high school and college, but in graduate school or in her career, her ability to create new ideas and implement them causes her to soar in achievement.[8]

How Can We Encourage Creative Ability?

Encourage children to undertake projects, like writing original computer programs, creating art projects, writing and illustrating their own books—whether they relate to school or not. Whatever their interests are, let them do creative work in that area and help them find interesting projects to do on their own.

For example, Sarah, Sternberg's daughter, is fascinated with science and had looked forward to entering the school science fair this year. However, her school decided not to have one. Her dad encouraged her to create her own project and enter it in the state science fair on her own. She jumped at the chance because it's her favorite interest. His son Seth set up his own computer networks on the home computer so that he can communicate with people all over the United States via computer. Sternberg's children came up with the ideas and Dad supported them, brainstormed with them, and helped them develop the ideas and gather materials. Saying "Try it; see what happens" or "That's a great idea!" can be a great encouragement to the creative thinker.

Encourage your child to save the raw materials of creation—odds and ends of stuff can be made into something else, a hodgepodge sculpture or an invention—and give him or her a space to explore and experiment. Gib, a creative guy who was very mechanical and insatiably curious about how things worked, was provided, by his parents, with many objects to take apart: small engines, a toaster, a coffeepot, even an old car. He progressed to putting them back together and fixing them. Now he is a graphic design major in college preparing for a career in advertising and perhaps commercial design.

Help your child set up a center for creative activity. Whether for artwork, for building rockets or woodworking, for dismantling and fixing old toasters or other machinery, or for whatever, this should be a place where your child can make a mess if it's part of the process. Don't expect kids to be perfectly neat and tidy while creating. Stock the creative center with Styrofoam packing, boxes, wood scraps, yarn, nails, buttons, seashells, pipe cleaners, and colored construction paper, in addition to paint, glue, and typical art supplies.

Encourage questions. Creative thinkers ask extraordinary questions: How does the heart work? How was that metal sculpture built? Encourage them! If one of your child's questions boggles your mind, respond, "That's a great question, but I don't know the answer!" Write it down on an index card, and next time you're at the library together, search for the answer. Some questions don't have one "right" answer; let your child think in an open-ended way about possibilities.

Take your child on outings. Take him or her to art galleries, to hands-on science museums, to see a research scientist work in his lab, or to watch a potter or other craftsperson at work. Cultivate whatever area your child expresses an interest in. And don't limit creativity to just the artistic fields—a person can be creative in music, in science and research, in problem solving, in writing, or in a host of other pursuits. Wherever your child's creativity shows itself, encourage it!

ANALYTICAL ABILITY

Analytical students like to get things done and follow rules and procedures. These students would rather follow the teacher's advice and method of analyzing literature than make up their own story. Travis is a whiz at test taking and scores high on standardized tests. Multiple-choice questions are his favorite in the classroom. His analytical, critical thinking has catapulted him to the top of his class. He is a detail person who thrives on solving complicated theorems in geometry and scored very high on the SAT for college entrance. Analytical skills like Travis's are valuable in business and industry, teaching and research, psychology and social issues, and math and science fields, to name just a few.

As a young student, the analytical child's questioning of everything will not necessarily make him or her the "student of the month." Some are downright argumentative in the classroom. Kyser, a Connecticut fifth grader, is curious about everything, and fortunately he has a dad who is willing to help him find out any information, discuss the wildest science ideas and questions, and even dive into projects, like constructing a dam or teaching him how to navigate with a compass.

How Can We Encourage Analytical Skills?

Emphasize analysis in parent-child interactions. "The best thing to do," Sternberg told me in a personal interview, "is when you interact with your children, give them reasons for what you're doing and encourage them to provide reasons for what they do." He and his children analyze politics, social issues, and things going on in their school, community, and lives on a regular basis. Talking with your children about *why* something happens and what they think about it encourages analytical thinking. Analyzing world events after you have watched the news together stimulates this kind of critical thinking.

Provide measuring tools and give your child problems to solve. A ruler, a compass, a map, a calculator, an egg timer, balance scales, thermometers, and a stopwatch are a good start. Ask questions like the following: How much carpet will it take to recarpet the living room? How can you find out if your new bookshelf will fit through the door into your room? How long will it take us to get to Grandma's at a speed of fifty-five miles per hour?

Provide opportunities for your child to conduct experiments. For example, here are two simple kitchen science projects:

- Egg Mysteries: Put a pint of water in two jars. Add eight tablespoons of salt to one jar and mix. Then put an egg in each jar. Ask why one egg sinks and one floats.
- Ocean in a Bottle: Mix a jar of food-colored water and half a jar of oil. Ask your child, "Why don't the water and oil mix?"

Stimulate curiosity around the kitchen by asking questions like: What happens to water when it boils? When cream is shaken hard?

Why does the banana decompose after many days on the kitchen counter?

Provide appropriate reading material. If your child is more interested in space, engines, and oceanography than the children's fiction and fantasy books that are read at school, get him or her books about those topics.

Encourage your child to collect various kinds of rocks, stamps, coins, or shells. Provide a shelf or plastic box with dividers for the collection. Analytical kids love to classify and categorize, and collections provide a great opportunity to use these skills.

PRACTICAL "STREET SMARTS"

Sternberg's third aspect of intelligence is what he calls "everyday" or practical intelligence, the ability to know what's required and to go ahead and do it right. This commonsense ability reminds me of a junior high student named Kim who was "street smart" in the sense of having a lot of practical, usable intelligence. She knew how to play the game—whether that game was classroom competition, how to get into the best college, or how to deal with people on her part-time job for a radio station. She made sure her activities contributed to a great application for the school she wanted acceptance to. She ran for student government and won. Kim has learned how to take her abilities and skills and apply them to the everyday tasks and problems of life. And she knows how to jump over obstacles. She made acceptable grades, but not top grades; however, she comes out on top because of her common sense and her ability to adapt to whatever environment she finds herself in. This student likes to compare and evaluate—whether that's an author's ideas and style in literature, or a politician's campaign promises.[9]

How Can We Encourage Practical Intelligence?

Get kids to interact with people. Part-time jobs, service projects, and full-time summer jobs when they are old enough are great ways to help children develop this ability. For example, Sternberg's son worked in his office in the summer and had to deal with people and be cooperative and interdependent with the research staff. Whether it's an entrepreneurial mowing business in the neighborhood during the summer or being a candy striper hospital volunteer, work experiences are great opportunities to develop practical intelligence.

Assign chores to your child at home, tasks that are important and benefit the whole family. Chores are "real-world stuff" that develop responsibility, adaptability, and the skill of doing things on time.

Show your child negotiating skills for resolving conflict with friends and family members. Instead of settling sibling arguments for your kids, help them find their own solution. "I see you're having trouble sharing Legos building blocks. Why don't you work out a plan? You could use this timer to have individual turns with the blocks and chart your schedule, cooperate and build something together, or you could think of another idea."

Help your child work independently. When your child has a history project or report to write, help him or her make a list of what is necessary to get it done on time, and a timetable or calendar to divide the task into doable bites. Brainstorm with the child to generate ideas and take him to the library or store for books and materials, but encourage him to work independently after you get him started rather than waiting until the last night and doing it for him.

WINNING WITH STRENGTHS

Whether it be creative, analytical, or practical intelligence—focus on what your child does best, and success will follow. Research at Gallup, Inc., an international research firm that studied more than 250,000 successful professionals in various fields, showed that the highest levels of achievement come when people are matched with activities that use their strengths. This study suggests that, instead of spending the majority of our time trying to correct weaknesses and remedy problem areas, *we should focus on our special talents.* "We estimate that for every one strength," wrote Donald Clifton and Paula Nelson, authors of *Soar with Your Strengths,* "we possess roughly one thousand nonstrengths. That ratio shows it would be a huge waste of energy to try to fix all of our weaknesses."[10]

In addition, one of the best ways to capitalize on your child's strengths is to pick one enjoyable area to pursue (instead of involving your child in a dozen lessons, athletic training programs, teams, and hobbies). From studies from the 1920s of over 1,440 highly gifted children, some who accomplished things in life and some who didn't, the research concluded that "what distinguished those of spectacular achievement from low achievement and failure was prudence and forethought, willpower, perseverance and desire. They chose among their many talents and concentrated their efforts."[11] Help your child develop goals and aspirations for the future and build on his or her strengths!

CHAPTER TEN

ANOTHER LOOK AT SMART: PART 2
MULTIPLE INTELLIGENCES

O nce there was a boy who consistently made a poor adjustment to school. In fact, in his senior year of secondary school he got a certificate from his doctor stating that he should leave school for six months. He was not a good all-around student, hated tests and exams, and did not make high grades. He had no school friends and his speech was delayed. Some teachers found him a problem and described him as dull. His father was ashamed of his lack of athletic ability. Who was he? The theoretical physicist and Nobel prize winner Albert Einstein, whose curiosity and perpetual sense of wonder lasted his whole life.[1]

Our narrow view of intelligence often keeps us from recognizing the abilities of children all around us. So let's look at a different perspective of the giftedness of people based on the research of Dr. Howard Gardner of Harvard University. In his book *Frames of Mind*, he says there are hundreds of ways to succeed and many different gifts and abilities to get you there. He feels that almost every child has strengths in at least one or more areas of intelligence (meaning abilities, talents, and mental skills) and describes these seven kinds of smarts. Although each intelligence is described individually below, in the real world a strength doesn't operate alone. Instead, a person usually has several areas of strength and talent working together. As Gardner says, "Intelligences work in concert."[2] Professional or vocational adult roles will involve a blending of several intelligences. And it is this *combination* or pattern of skills that enables a person to function or succeed in a profession or artistic endeavor. A design engineer for NASA, for example, would likely possess spatial talent and logical-mathematical intelligence. A politician might be linguistically and logically intelligent and have strong people skills. Succeeding as a dance performer and instructor requires kinesthetic, musical, and interpersonal talent.[3]

The development of these intelligences may be more important than some of the issues we put so much emphasis on during the school years. Yes, classwork is important, good grades are important, and high standardized test scores are a blessing! But research shows that IQ and other standardized tests are poor predictors of success and achievement in life. They can predict school performance itself, but there is only a small correlation between high grades and achievement in the real world.

For example, in my high school graduating class, there were many different abilities and achievement levels—and a variety of outcomes and careers in our adult lives. One girl, with straight A's throughout elementary and secondary school and voted "most likely to succeed," has worked for years as a secretary at a law firm. An average-achieving guy I knew who had strong personal intelligence and language talent became a successful psychologist, family counselor, and seminar speaker. One of my friends, a bright English student, became a Hollywood scriptwriter and producer. And another, a below average student, and thought of as an unmotivated "underachiever" in school, is now an extremely successful owner and general manager of a large metropolitan car dealership. She uses her strengths in the business world in delegating responsibility, working with people, promotion, and sales. One of our brightest science students, considered in his youth a "genius," who garnered a doctorate from a major institution, doesn't work or do anything productive. But another "test-smart" young woman turned her talents to build a megachain of wildly successful record stores, engage in investments, and buy a newspaper. Other average students I knew have become successful hospital administrators, vice presidents of corporations, and an award-winning science teacher in our state. What mattered for each of us was finding our strengths and capitalizing on them!

DISCOVERING DIFFERENT KINDS OF SMARTS

Two kinds of intelligence—logical-mathematical and linguistic (or language talent)—are readily identified on standardized tests and affirmed in the classroom, but the other five areas of gifts do not show up on pencil-and-paper tests and often are not spotted by teachers. Here are Dr. Gardner's classifications and how to discover, encourage, and develop your child's unique gifts.

Spatial Intelligence

Spatial ability means being able to visualize an object in your mind's eye, and even imagine how it would look if it were turned around. Children who are spatially gifted are great at visualizing pictures, objects, and even how things work in their mind. These children can find their way around a city, a ski area, or a large, multifloored building with ease. They notice fine details,[4] and can see something once and reproduce it on paper—and thus possess artistic or design ability. They may love to draw, enjoy complicated puzzles, or design rocket ships and clay creations (depending on their interests).

The spatial abilities are not something these people conjure up; instead, they are just a part of their thinking. "My own hunch about strong intellectual abilities is that an individual so blessed does not merely have an easy time learning new patterns; he in fact learns them so readily that it is virtually impossible for him to forget them. The simple melodies continue to play on in his mind, the sentences linger there, the spatial or gestural configurations are readily brought to the fore, although they may not have been tapped for a while," says Gardner.[5] In other words, in the case of spatially intelligent people, these visual abilities are so interwoven with their thinking that they are quite natural and easily accessed.

Brian Jones, a young man born deaf, doesn't need to hear to create three-dimensional models of buildings for large companies. He has excellent spatial talent, three-dimensional conception, and a sharp attention to detail. Despite being hearing-impaired, he is pursuing a successful career in drafting. Even as a child he noticed models of buildings in magazines and on trips to downtown and paid careful attention to the structure. Like many spatially talented people, he has a vivid imagination. Brian's future looks bright because he has found a career area that focuses on his strength. Spatially gifted people can become architects, sculptors, artists, or design engineers.

Here are some ways to develop spatial talent:

- Provide markers, paper, charcoal, brushes, an easel, and other art materials.
- Provide games like checkers, chess, three-dimensional tic-tac-toe; and computer graphics programs like Paintbrush or Picturewriter.
- Origami, the Japanese art of paper folding, is a wonderful way to learn about the many possible relationships between different shapes. Children can make birds, giraffes, boats, or party hats out of the origami paper (instruction books with colorful paper are available at children's bookstores and craft shops).
- Tangrams are two-dimensional geometric pieces (such as squares, triangles, rectangles) that can be arranged to make formations and shapes like animals or houses or to fit in a tangram puzzle book. Spatially talented kids love the challenge of tangram puzzles.
- Encourage projects like assembling models of airplanes or rockets, or inventing things. Most important, follow your child's interests, whether that is map-making or art, paper airplanes or exploring the neighborhood park surroundings.

When Tom Lough's son, Kyser, saw a diagram of a dam in the encyclopedia, he wanted to make one and asked his dad to help. They got the needed supplies, worked on the dam project on Saturdays, and before long had the waterwheels operating. Kyser was so proud of the dam he had built that they videotaped it while working, and sent a copy of the tape to his grandparents.

Musical Intelligence

A good clue to a musically gifted child is perfect pitch at a very early age.[6] Luciano Pavarotti, one of the world's greatest opera singers, showed musical talent from age four. As a child he had an excellent alto voice. He listened constantly to his family's big record collection and regularly heard his father sing in their local church.[7] In addition, the musically intelligent child can imitate tone, rhythm, and melody, and thus remember and sing songs from hearing them once or twice. Although all children have some musical aptitude, this child has what we call a high music IQ. John Tesh, television anchor/reporter and co-host of "Entertainment Tonight," has high musical intelligence. At six years old, he was playing classical piano. At ten, he began studying trumpet and trombone at The Juilliard School. His compositions include many themes for international sports programs and television programs; he has won two Emmy awards for his musical compositions and produced eight albums.

Here are some ways to encourage your musically gifted child:

- For young children, provide rhythm instruments and chances to sing, clap, and play along to music tapes with the instruments. For the preschooler, music should be a lot of fun. Sing to and with the child around the house. (Don't push a child into formal music lessons too early just because he or she seems to have talent; some teachers recommend waiting until the child is seven or eight and requests an instrument and lessons before you sign up.)
- Play a variety of good music at home and in the car, including classical music, folk music, traditional children's music, and the best Broadway scores and movie sound tracks.
- If you have a home computer, a software program that allows your child to write and perform original music is a great resource. With one program, Songwriter, the child

can experiment with time and melody to create single-voice compositions. With others, the child can print out the score of an original song.

■ Take your child to symphony concerts, live musical theater, and other musical events in your community.

■ For children who love to sing, karaoke tapes and a microphone are great fun. The karaoke tape has the background music and provides the words, and your child can sing along and perform his or her favorite tunes.

■ Many more ideas for picking the right instrument for your child, encouraging practice without burnout, and developing musical intelligence are in my book *How to Grow a Young Music Lover* (Harold Shaw Publishers, 1994).

Bodily Kinesthetic Intelligence

Children with kinesthetic talent can coordinate muscle movements, operate with grace and timing, and use their body and other objects with skill and precision. These children are usually standouts in athletics, drama, mechanics, or any hands-on endeavor. The computer inside their brain coordinates their movements, their abundant energy, and their grace—all of which are evident at an early age.

Greg Louganis, winner of several Olympic gold medals for diving, possessed amazing precision and kinesthetic talent. Like many bodily kinesthetic people, he also had difficulty learning to read. But he excelled in anything athletic and was particularly successful in diving.

The main skill some kinesthetically talented people possess is in manipulating things, not fixing things. Paul could drive a car from an early age, and years before he was old enough, longed for his pilot's license. Very coordinated in sports, he can't repair the family dishwasher or plumbing, but after only a few pilot's lessons he could fly an airplane. At one point, his instructor covered up the dials and said, "Fly this plane at an airspeed of exactly eighty miles per hour." Without any difficulty, Paul was able to feel how fast he was going, fly the plane by instruments, and when his instructor took the clipboard off the dial, he was exactly on the correct speed.

This ability to "feel," dexterity, and coordination make kinesthetically intelligent people excellent actors, dancers, professional baseball pitchers, computer technicians, and sometimes, mechanics and brain surgeons.

Here are some ways to enhance this skill:

- Give your child opportunities to explore different sports to find one that he or she can enjoy or excel in. Consider team sports like soccer, basketball, or hockey, or individual ones like gymnastics, tennis, or cross-country running. What's important is finding a physical activity your child enjoys and developing skills in that area.
- Provide things to take apart and a toolbox with pliers, screwdriver, hammer, wrench, etc. Old clocks and electric toys found at garage sales are fun to dissect and "fix." Your child may eventually be able to repair your television or other household machines like my friend's kinesthetically talented son Chase (they've made some great savings on repair bills).
- Provide opportunities to see a variety of athletic events in the community, from dance recitals to swim meets to horseback riding competitions to Olympic festivals.

Logical-Mathematical Talent

Children with logical-mathematical talent are fascinated with numbers, order, sequencing, and counting. They tend to be curious, ask searching (and sometimes irritating) questions, and have intense concentration even at an early age. They show early computational skills, so they tend to be whizzes in math, and are excellent at problem solving. Remember that, sometimes, negative qualities in children are actually signs of gifts. These kids' ability to logically analyze everything can cause them to be argumentative at home or in the classroom, so working on social skills, being considerate of others even when they disagree or think others are wrong, will go a long way toward helping them adapt to different situations.

As a child, Tom Lough was extremely frustrated in his science and math courses. It was tough for teachers to make the material interesting and challenging enough, and he consistently asked questions they couldn't answer. He was curious about everything from the origin of the constellations to how a muscle really works. School science was taught by rote and included few experiments. Fortunately, his parents bought him a set of encyclopedias that he read for pleasure about any subject that interested him. Although he wasn't challenged in school, his interest in science continued to grow due to highlights like outings with his dad, an amateur astronomer, to watch meteor showers and constellations, and discussions with two uncles, superb tinkerers who talked in detail about their attempts to create a perpetual-motion machine and a solar house. He entered a science fair competition with a three-dimensional model of his personal theory on how the planets were formed and took honorable mention. Tom went on to get a bachelor's degree in engineering from West Point, a master's in geodetic science, a master's in physics, a doctorate in educational psychology, and is now curriculum coordinator for Lego/Dacta. He helps develop new computerized and electronic building kits and products, is a computer expert, and is working on a master's in business administration.

Stimulate your child's logical-math intelligence by:

- Providing hands-on science projects, whether it's stargazing in the back yard and identifying constellations with a star map from a nearby planetarium, or collecting and labeling different kinds of insects and butterflies.
- Providing computer games that use strategy and focus on problem solving.
- Playing games like Mastermind and Foursquare that develop logic and math skills. Battleship, Monopoly, chess, and math puzzle books require strategy and problem-solving skills.
- Reading about scientists. Subscribe to Science-by-Mail, a Boston Museum of Science program in which children do science experiments, the results of which are evaluated by a real scientist, who corresponds with the children and gives them suggestions for further exploration. (See

appendix for address and phone number, page 192.)

- Giving opportunities for your child to learn basic accounting skills. Provide a ledger book so that your child can set up a budget and keep track of money from gifts, allowance, and work projects. Let the child handle the money for your neighborhood garage sale, or create a money-making project for Christmas vacation or summer.
- Watching television specials on oceanography, space and aviation, and other science and nature topics.
- Accelerating math progress. If your child is advanced in math and thus bored with the level of math at school, challenge him or her outside of class. When sixth grader Philip was doing well on his math exams but failing math because he skipped the homework he found boring, his mother hired a college student to teach him algebra, but persuaded him to do his homework to keep his teacher happy. There are many summer math and science programs for children gifted in this area at colleges and universities around the country.

Linguistic Intelligence

Language-talented children talk early and are fascinated with the sound and meaning of words. They express their verbal ability by telling descriptive stories, remembering commercials word for word, and enjoying wordplay like tongue twisters and puns. Generally, these children love reading and being read to, and from reading experiences at both school and home, rapidly build a large vocabulary.

Ann excelled in language arts throughout elementary school, and took all the honors and advanced placement courses offered in English and history in high school. A prodigious reader, she placed out of two years of college English because of her own at-home reading of the classics, in addition to her honors courses. Although quiet, she loved to write, and became the editor of her college newspaper, entered law school at twenty, and plans to work as a political journalist for a large city newspaper. Although she was frustrated with math, and has a hard time finding her way around a new city, she's a whiz with words, creative in her expression, and loves the challenge of a new article to research.

Here's how to encourage your linguistically talented child:

- From the stories your preschooler dictates to you and you put together into a book, to longer fantasies and tales your school-age child writes, value your child's expression. Encourage him or her to make personal greeting cards, to write a family newsletter, to write scripts for plays and perform them with friends.
- For a birthday or Christmas, buy a blank book and have your child write down ideas, poems, travel experiences, and stories in a journal. Journal keeping is some of the best practice for developing writing skills.
- Play word games like Scrabble, Password, Scattergories, charades (pantomiming words, book titles, and movie titles). Make up rhymes, limericks, and tongue twisters, and have fun with language.
- Provide a variety of wonderful books—classics like *Winnie the Pooh*, *The Wizard of Oz*, and C. S. Lewis's *Chronicles of Narnia*—and read aloud as a family. Provide recorded books for car trips and place books by your child's bed to read at bedtime.
- Encourage your child to write letters, to send thank-you notes for gifts, and to correspond with pen pals in other countries. Ask a distant relative or close friend to agree to regularly correspond with your child.
- If your child writes a promising poem or story, help her submit it to a children's or teen's magazine for possible publication. There are over 150 young people's magazines that publish children's writing. (See appendix, pages 190 and 194.)

The Personal Intelligences

The personal intelligences include "interpersonal" talent, or people skills, which enables a child even from an early age to understand the feelings of others, to communicate with them, and to lead in a group. In the neighborhood, the personally intelligent child is the one who says, "Let's round up all our Christmas trees, put them together, and make a tree fort. I'll get some rope, you help me carry our tree, and we'll get started!" This child's enthusiasm is contagious; he or she is skilled at making unconnected kids join in with the project. Our son Justin has strong interpersonal skills—he is sociable, friendships are important to him, and he can get along with people and express himself in almost any situation.

You can encourage people skills by:

■ Giving your child leadership opportunities at home and church, or for the neighborhood block party. For example, put your child in charge of a project within his or her ability level, like planning and coordinating the family campout, his or her birthday party, or a fund-raising project for a local charity.
■ Encouraging your child in speech, debate, and student government activities at school.
■ Encouraging dramatic role-playing when reading. This helps your child identify with and empathize with different characters.
■ Directing your child toward a good organization like Scouts, 4-H, or a church youth group, where he or she can learn the dynamics of group activities and interact and work with different kinds of people toward common goals.
■ Suggest your child or teen start a business, such as lawn mowing, dog watching or walking, car washing and detailing, house sitting, catering, or another endeavor.

The second kind of personal intelligence is called "intra-personal" skill, which is a big word for knowing one's own abilities and feelings. Children with this intelligence are intuitive, reflective children who like to work on projects independently, and are opinionated at an early age. The best way to encourage these kids' talent (which is often blended with at least one or two other intelligences, such as logical-math or spatial) is to give them opportunities to pursue their own special interests. If one such child is interested in dinosaurs, let the child read up on them, take a trip to the local museum dinosaur exhibit, and perhaps write for more information from other museums. The child could keep a notebook with his or her writings about dinosaurs, pictures the child has found, and information from encyclopedias. Young people with intra-personal intelligence love to do independent research, collect information, and do experiments and personal projects.

▽

If you are puzzled about what your child's gifts might be, listen, ask questions, and watch what your child takes the most pride in and what sparks him or her, whether at school or at home. Ask: What do you like to do most of all? What are you good at? What do you enjoy doing at school? Your child's answers are a clue to abilities and strengths you can help him or her develop.

A child may have individual strengths—such as empathy, which is needed by nurses, physical therapists, and others in the caring professions; or nurturing abilities, which can help make great teachers, parents, and managers; or perception, which novel writers and artists possess.[8]

If you look at your child with an eye to the possibilities, you can even see strengths in the "negatives" of children: the "daydreamer" may be a creative thinker or an inventor; the bossy child often has administrative ability that can put him in charge of his own company someday; the student who balks at directions and finds different ways to do things might be a creative thinker; the one who is always challenging your opinions may have valuable logical and analytical ability when she "grows into" her gift. In the meantime, be patient and remind yourself to look at the *donut* (what he does well) instead of the *hole* (what he lacks or does poorly).

In addition, use your child's talents to spark study for school subjects. If she is musical, find someone who can show her how to set information to be tested over to *music*. If she is analytical, suggest she put information to be learned in a *logical order*. If she is artistically talented, have her add *illustrations* to help her remember material.

As you nurture your child's hidden talent, your child will grow in confidence and self-esteem. He or she will develop motivation to tackle more difficult assignments and jobs at school. Later you can help your child develop goals and focus on what he or she wants to do in summer vacations, after-school activities, in later education, and in life. You can help the child pursue opportunities to develop strengths, and encourage hard work and practice. Those "hidden talents" can become a great source of joy and direction.

CHAPTER ELEVEN

YOUR CHILD IN THE CLASSROOM
HANDLING WEAKNESSES SO THEY DON'T BLOCK STRENGTHS

A re we setting students up for success or for failure?

A teacher's instructional style can have a major effect on how a child performs in his or her classroom. It all depends on the teacher's strengths and weaknesses and the student's strengths and weaknesses. As hard as we teachers try, we tend to teach right out of our own learning style—especially under time pressure when there's a lot of material to get across. Some teachers prefer a quiet environment in the classroom and assign a lot of silent reading. Others do an abundance of talking and explaining to get concepts across to their class. And many have a hard time with an active student who needs some movement while learning.

Yet a surefire way to stifle learning for the visual student is to say everything aloud, rapidly, and not to write any information on the board. For the auditory student, saying "Shhh!" having a no-talking-while-learning rule, prohibiting questions, and mandating that all reading be silent can produce problems. For the kinesthetic/tactile child, saying "Be still! No moving! Stay in your seat!" and "Stop drumming your fingers!" combined with all pencil-and-paper assignments and little or no hands-on learning is a sure deterrent to learning. When your child has a teacher whose teaching style is just the opposite of his way of receiving information, the mix-match can have a big impact on school performance. Let's look at some typical teaching-style patterns below.

AUDITORY/VERBAL TEACHING

I remember my first teaching assignment at North Junior High School in Waco, Texas. Fresh out of college, I was a little nervous but ready for the big day! Twenty-seven sweaty ninth-grade boys just out of gym class filed in to fill the rows in front of my desk. I had the students introduce themselves (and quickly realized who the class clowns were). Then I began introducing the American history course we were going to embark on, the units of study, and the special events and speakers of the semester. My forty minutes of well-prepared, enthusiastic verbal introduction and directions, however, did not get rave reviews from these teens!

Although I did hand out a typed syllabus, or outline of the course, with classroom guidelines and such, the visual guys started doodling on it after fifteen minutes. The auditory ones gave good eye contact and asked a few questions. The "movers" were fidgety, flicking pencils (and one, his lighter); a few got up to sharpen pencils right while I was talking, and most were totally tuned out after a few minutes of my talking. One six-foot-tall boy, who had gotten out of the juvenile detention center the night before, fell asleep. I quickly found that not only for *their* sakes, but for my survival, I needed to make extra effort to use visuals, outline ideas on the board, and most of all, get them actively involved in the material with projects and hands-on activities to facilitate learning. What a challenge that year was!

You see, being an auditory learner, my style of teaching was very auditory/verbal. When teaching English, I explained a lot, encouraged class discussions, and frequently asked for feedback. Students had assigned reading, which we discussed. They wrote in reading journals. I asked them oral questions to see if they understood the concepts. Several times a week I gave lectures on the material and the students took notes. Sometimes I let students study together and ask each other questions to prepare for a test. Tests were typed and always included essay questions. But sometimes I gave a pop quiz in which I called out questions and they wrote the answers. They also had small group activities, projects, and discussions with specific objectives.

Bulletin boards were not my forte. Although I did usually have the corkboard covered with something—sometimes the students' work—it was not the center of our learning excitement! (Fortunately, a high school room usually has only one bulletin board—in contrast to an elementary classroom's four or five.) I found an overhead projector more cumbersome than useful (although I now use one in large-group teacher seminars I present). Whenever possible, I assigned art projects related to our units of study and had guest speakers when it would enhance our learning. I had the students tape-record "on the scene" interviews with characters from literature and history. I really had to brainstorm to come up with activities outside the reading-writing-discussion mode, and found team teaching a benefit for the students because the best of both of our modalities was brought into the instruction.

VISUAL TEACHING

Gordon, a visual teacher, has a neat, organized third-grade classroom. There are bulletin boards on each wall of the room. Each one is brightly decorated—one with a seasonal theme, two with themes related to current topics of study—and these are changed frequently. Desks are in straight rows in front of Gordon's desk. There are several learning centers highlighted by attention-getting artwork. At open house, this teacher's classroom is a big hit. As a parent, you can see he put a lot of time and effort into making a creative physical environment for the students. (One social studies teacher's room I sat in during open house had so many pictures of people they were studying, posters of historical events, a huge time line, and other visuals covering the walls that I couldn't concentrate on what she was saying.)

Gordon always has the schedule for the day and directions written on the board or on task cards for the students. He assigns seat work for workbook assignments and handout work sheets. Reading is frequently done silently, stressing a sight-word approach, context clues, and pictures. Stories written and illustrated by students are backed with construction paper and displayed neatly in the hall. He often shows an educational video or filmstrip. Art activities are frequent, and parents loved the "All About Me" book each received for Christmas with photos of their child growing up and the child's narration underneath.

In math drill time, students use flash cards to practice their basic math facts and do work sheets. They make spelling flash cards to drill with also. He is very prompt with his grading, and students receive a computer-generated summary of their performance every week to take home. No guesswork here! Gordon's strong organizational skills give a sense of security and order to the children in his classroom, and parents appreciate his consistency in keeping them informed. Each student's work sheets and written work go in folders in a large stand-up file on the counter by the teacher's desk, where they will go home in the "Friday folder" at the end of the week.

KINESTHETIC/TACTILE TEACHING

Judy, the kinesthetic teacher, whose second dominant modality is auditory and who is very musical, has a classroom that reflects her interactive, hands-on teaching style. On one wall is a clown named Willy, juggling yellow, pink, and orange fluorescent balls with the students' names in cursive. A large banner on the west wall says "KIDS ARE SPECIAL." Another bulletin board in this fourth-grade classroom has close-up photos of insects, spiders, praying mantises, and the like. Another bulletin board has a large turkey the children helped make. Each child took a paper feather off the bird, wrote on it the name of someone he or she was thankful for, and put it back on the turkey's wings and tail. The east board has photos and a newspaper article of Judy's clown-camp experience. It's very personal. And Judy is a very person-centered teacher who shares her life with her students.

Desks are in the middle of the room in rows, but are moved often so the class can do a lot of floor work and group work. Yesterday, for instance, they were studying calendars, and each child made a calendar for the next five months. Twenty-two students (and teacher) sat on the floor assembling the calendars with poster board and markers. They posted each other's birthdays and holidays and decorated them.

Before Judy introduced multiplication to the class, she realized they were scared it was going to be too hard for them. So she came in as a cowboy character named Howdy Dowdy, and shared with them in a humorous way all about multiplication. "I have two cousins, Addeee and Multiii. Now when Addeee adds numbers up she gets tired, but with Multiii it's like going from walking to flying!" Then she showed them physically with manipulatives what multiplication is, and the next day they did a work sheet.

Judy, nicknamed "Sparky" by her college speech class, always tries to have the students apply what they're learning to the world around them. They do many science experiments, and she takes them on field trips whenever she can. After an aerospace and aviation week last year—for which she got a national grant and brought in the Oklahoma State University Flying Aggies and other aviation experts from all over the state—she took fifty children to the Aerospace Academy at the University of Oklahoma, where they made and shot off rockets, and made and used telescopes. Writing and reading are also linked with the real world: this week they were making and writing get-well greeting cards to an Olympic skater who was injured. Paper dolls of the book character Flat Stanley were sent around the world with their letters, and they are awaiting their return.

The open shelves contain many hands-on materials, which students take to their desks to create their own mini-learning centers. Art in Judy's classroom means doing pottery and multi-texture collages. When they listened to Shel Silverstein's poetry on tape, they each memorized one of his poems, and she videotaped their individual recitals for the class to watch later. If a student asks a good question she can't answer, they stop what they are doing and look it up. When they do addition and subtraction, she simulates a class trip to Six Flags Over Texas, they figure the costs on the board, and then compare it to the costs for their individual family to go. The whole class looks forward to the day in May when their teacher is going to introduce her clown character, Sonshine Joy, and teach them to put on clown makeup.

STRENGTHS AND WEAKNESSES

Each of these teachers has strengths and weaknesses and addresses students' needs in different ways. Gordon's orderly, step-by-step approach and visual style is supportive for visual kids with analytic thinking styles who thrive on structure. There may be students in his classroom who need more explanation or reading aloud than he does. My auditory style was fine for the very verbal high school student who was an avid reader, writer, and discusser, and helpful for the student who needed a lot of explanation to understand concepts. But the strongly visual or kinesthetic student was frustrated unless I provided plenty of visuals and for-credit alternative projects, instead of grading only written reports or tests.

Judy's spontaneity and hands-on teaching is a wonderful (and rare) opportunity for her tactile and kinesthetic students. Her "open" classroom tends to have more activity, and a buzzing noise level—although under complete control—can be distracting to some kids. And actually, research shows that most children, regardless of learning style, whether gifted or average, do better if hands-on activities are included, especially up through age twelve when they are in the "concrete" developmental learning stage.

However, only a small minority of teachers show a preference for hands-on/tactile-kinesthetic learning, and often these individuals become kindergarten, art, science, music, or technical-education teachers or become coaches. A survey of more than nine thousand teachers showed they had an 85–90 percent preference for visual learning. The secondary preference was auditory, and looking and listening was the main pattern of their teaching.[1] Moreover, research shows teachers (even college faculty) tend to give higher evaluations and grades to students who match their own cognitive styles.[2]

Note how the organization, instruction, activities, and environment in each of the classrooms above are affected by the teacher's learning/instructional style. Hopefully your child's teachers will take into account the differences in students and direct their teaching toward all modalities. Perhaps they have been trained to plan lessons carefully so that every kind of learner is included. When there is a real conflict between teaching and learning styles, as when, for instance, the teacher presents everything in a part-to-whole, step-by-step way and the student is a "global" thinker who needs the big picture; or when visual or kinesthetic learners are handicapped by a teacher who uses the lecture method exclusively; "friends become enemies, misunderstandings flourish, and learning withers," says Dr. Priscilla Vail.[3]

WORKING WITH THE TEACHER

How can children's different learning needs be met and strengths built on in a classroom with over twenty children? If you or I had twenty-five children at home, we couldn't instruct each individually any more than a teacher could in a classroom. (However, one of the advantages of home-schooling is that with just one or a few children you can individualize and teach to the child's strength.)

With forty-five-minute classes in the normal middle school— fifteen of which are taken up with taking attendance, paperwork, and settling kids down—and with trying to teach children with a broad range of abilities and developmental stages, teachers have their hands full! That's why I feel learning-style information is some of the best news for parents and students. Although you can't completely change the teacher's style any more than you can change the child's learning style, you can:

- Make the teacher aware of the child's learning style, but don't expect him or her to change the whole class instruction and procedure just for your child.
- Ask for modifications that will help your child succeed and learn. It is especially important to find a strategy to bypass or *manage*[4] a weakness that intrudes on your child's productivity, hinders achievement, or reduces his self-concept.

- Teach your child to adapt and compensate.
- Show your child how to change the information, whenever possible, into a form that his or her brain best comprehends and remembers.

How can you work with teachers—without alienating them—when modifications for a child's learning style need to be made? Here are some tips:

- Start at the beginning of the school year. Try to head off any problems *before* the child starts failing or becomes so frustrated that he or she acts out and his or her behavior deteriorates. The purpose is not to share negative information, but to open up communication.
- Have a conference with the teacher. You could say, "This is what we've seen in the past and what we're working on. Sometimes Matt has a hard time focusing in on the instruction and dealing with distractions if he's in the back of the room. Could you seat him close to the front? We'd very much appreciate it. And if there's a problem, please let us know right away."
- Children don't have to be certified "learning disabled" to have modifications made in the classroom. In fact, it can be better *not* to have them given a negative label if support can be provided and small modifications made. Nine times out of ten, if teachers are approached graciously, they will make modifications. They want the child to succeed too! (Even if a student is certified "learning disabled" and has an Individualized Education Plan [IEP], parents need to check with the school periodically and make sure the support is being provided and the provisions for the student are being carried out. Don't assume everything is taken care of. No one can be your child's advocate for the long term but you.) In the process, don't make excuses for the child or take over his or her homework responsibilities.

As Marilyn Morgan, a veteran teacher, says, "Don't handicap your child by making excuses for him or by telling him, 'You can't do this.' We have a whole generation of students who have had excuses made for them and haven't learned to compensate, initiate and put out effort to overcome their obstacles, or use their strengths in the regular classroom. We often take all the responsibility for learning away from the child."

Be careful that when you ask for a change, it is to empower and equip your child, to bypass a weakness and thus help your child succeed, *not* to take responsibilities or challenges away from him or her. The student needs to show initiative and put out effort to compensate and learn. Insist that your child show interest by coming in for extra help when needed and asking the teacher for help when he or she doesn't understand something.

If you can volunteer in the classroom, you'll find new ways to support your child's homework and study. In addition, the teacher is usually more open to your input and suggestions. Kathy, mother of four boys, two of whom have some learning problems, says helping in her sons' classes is one of the most valuable things she's done. She learned what the expectations and homework requirements were like, she saw ways she could assist them at home, and her relationship with the teacher grew. "Besides, I love being a part of their world," said Kathy. When you volunteer and see what's going on in the classroom, you can head off problems before they become serious.

One year Kathy's second grader began saying, "Couldn't I just stay home today?" each morning. That week as she observed the class while assisting in the back of the room, she realized the problem was that he was very bored with the work. She shared this with his teacher and said she'd appreciate it if she could challenge him and enrich the curriculum for him. The teacher agreed to do that and offered ways Kathy could challenge him at home.

MAKING MODIFICATIONS—OVERCOMING WEAKNESSES

When there is a conflict between the teacher's style and the learner's style, or when the student has a weakness that is hindering learning, there are many possibilities to remedy the situation. What we need to keep in mind is: Are we setting the student up for success or for failure? Very observant teachers may intuitively make the changes, or they may need the suggestions of parents, tutors, or the student himself or herself. If a teacher knows where a student is apt to encounter difficulties, the teacher can help the child deal with it. Here is an example.

Keisha, a ninth grader, was having trouble passing in science class, so her mother got a tutor for her. But her greater problem was the migraine headaches she was having, that the doctor attributed to "stress." In fact, she had missed thirteen days of the nine weeks due to severe headaches. Her mother had tried to help, but was frustrated with her daughter's failing science grades and had been after her every night to study harder. After some evaluation and dialogue with Keisha, her tutor began to see the underlying problem. Every day in science class the students had to take notes while the teacher talked, lectured, and wrote everything on the board—quickly, I might add! When Keisha had to listen and try to follow the lecture, write notes from the board, spell correctly, and remember all at the same time, the fuses blew; she became frustrated and overwhelmed, and a migraine often resulted.

Since the notes were necessary to succeeding in the class, parent, tutor, and teacher worked out an alternative plan: the teacher had Keisha listen while he lectured and wrote on the board. She could listen much better when not writing, as the auditory modality was her strength. Then she was permitted to hand-copy another student's notes after class. That afternoon, when she went home to study, she read her notes into a tape recorder and played them back later to review. She began making B's and C's instead of F's, and best of all, didn't miss any school that marking period due to migraines.

Here are some other modifications that can be made to facilitate students' learning, to manage and compensate for weaknesses, and to build on strengths:

A lap-top computer for word processing in the classroom. All students need typing and keyboard skills, but especially those who have difficulty with handwriting or the *output* of information. If a student's fine motor skills are not developed enough to permit fast, neat penmanship, or if a student is very tactile and kinesthetic, or has some memory problems, a word processor is a lifesaving tool for writing reports, recording class notes, etc. As Dr. Mel Levine says, "A word processor is like an extra memory. Kids who have some memory problems might find that a word processor really improves their ability to write."[5] Of course, if the word processor has a spell-check capacity, that helps students with spelling problems. The teacher accepting work typed on a computer at home can also be a big help.

Modifying for movement. Kinesthetic learners who have a need for movement and for whom "sitting still" can take all their concentration can be helped by having two desks. One teacher shared with me that for one of her students, this modification made a terrific improvement in behavior and focus. When the student began to lose concentration, she could move to the other chair, quietly, not disturbing others. The teacher also had her pass out papers and tests and deliver notes to the office, which gave her further opportunities to move (and help at the same time).

Rocking, pedaling, and reading. Innovative teachers have provided a few beanbag chairs and a big rug in a comfortable "reading center," a rocking chair to read in (the rocking movement helps some students concentrate), or a stationary bike with a stand to hold a book, in which a student can pedal and read. One teacher who allowed his reading-troubled "movers" to pedal and read found it made a big difference in comprehension and interest. J. C., one of the students, said, "When I got up there, when I started to read, it was like a miracle. I started laughing because I couldn't help it, because I was reading almost one-hundred percent better."[6]

Class seating. For easily distracted students, or students whose concentration seems to wander when they sit in the back, sitting close to the front of the room can help them concentrate. Visual learners also do better when seated close to the front. Auditory students who are distracted by sounds and have trouble filtering out noise when trying to concentrate can be seated where they can hear without being distracted (for example, by the door where people are passing in the hall would not be an ideal place). A student who needs quiet to concentrate while reading or studying in the classroom could also try a "dead" Walkman headset (one without any music playing).

Visual aids. If the teacher lectures a lot, a graphic accompaniment should be provided for a visual learner, especially if auditory processing is weak or delayed. Either an outline on the board or a partially blank copy of the teacher's outline for the student to take notes on and fill in, greatly aids learning. Using visual methods like mind mapping (or webbing, clustering) on the board or overhead transparencies, diagrams, and charts will also benefit these students.

Tape recorder. Brad is a bright auditory learner in the sixth grade who has trouble taking class notes and following directions due to some delay in fine motor-skills development. He takes a small tape recorder to every class and tape-records teacher presentations and instructions for assignments, and then reviews these at home before doing his homework. He also has two of his textbooks on tape to listen to as he reads. Students whose reading level is deficient can qualify for Books on Tape through the Library of Congress, and get novels and textbooks on tape to aid their learning.

A tape recorder is also helpful to dictate the student's ideas into or tell a story into before writing it, for making "fill-in-the-blank" study tapes, and other review. (See chapter 5 for examples.) For a student who needs to hear test questions in addition to seeing them, the test can be read aloud or tape-recorded, with the student writing the answers on the test paper or giving them on tape.

Class discussions. Some students "freeze up" when randomly called on in class to answer questions. They may know the information, but when put on the spot they experience anxiety or can't think of the words fast enough. This kind of problem can be greatly helped with some communication and an agreement between teacher and student. For Mary, that meant the teacher didn't call on her unless her hand was up to volunteer an answer. Another teacher agreed to not call on a student until she was standing in front of her desk to "cue" her. In another classroom, the agreement was that the teacher would call on Beau only for questions that could be answered with yes or no for the first few weeks of school.

Colored transparency sheets. For some students with low visual strengths, a colored transparency in a rose or teal color, kept at their desks to cover a page of print with, reduces glare and enables them to read much better.

Timed tests. For some students, the pressure of timed tests causes such anxiety that they forget all they studied and actually knew of the material. Others just need more time to get their ideas down on paper. Allowing extra time on tests can greatly help these students.

Teach a different way each day. Teachers introducing an entirely new concept, like the reproductive parts of a flower and how that connects to genetics, could teach to a different modality each day. The first day the teacher introduces the subject in a hands-on way (dissecting the flowers on white paper and identifying the parts); the next day the teacher draws diagrams of the flower and labels the parts (visual and kinesthetic); and the next day is devoted to reading aloud from the science book and to groups making clusters on big butcher paper of everything they've learned about flowers (auditory and visual).

Different products for different learners. Another way for teachers to address the learning styles of students and modify their approach is by allowing different learners to choose different "products," or results, which will be evaluated for a grade.

For example, in lieu of a written composition on a chapter of science or history, a kinesthetic student could produce a diorama; devise and set up an experiment; or make a learning center, relief map, educational game, or mobile. A visual student could make a poster, produce a videotape or filmstrip, or create a time line or advertising brochure for the class. An auditory student could produce and record a radio commentary; make an oral presentation to the class; or write a newspaper article, journal entry, or speech.[7] Three students of different learning strengths could combine talents and produce a documentary videotape on a subject. All students can use a computer to do products and projects. In one middle-school science classroom I visited, groups of students were taking a simulated space trip on computer, figuring speed, doing mathematical calculations, and recording their results on the word processor to print out.

In lieu of a week of final exams in our son's high school in

Yarmouth, Maine, tenth- and eleventh-grade students had a real-life experience: shadowing a person in a career, working with the person, asking questions about the education and training necessary for the position, and writing a journal every day about their experiences and observations. For many of the students, our son included, this real-life activity was one of the most valuable of the year, and they gained some goals and aspirations from the mentoring experience.

Whether it's providing a calculator or something as small as manipulatives to help in math class, or a "dead" Walkman to drown out noise, when we support students, address their learning needs, and help them manage and compensate for their weaknesses, we can make a big difference in their motivation, reduce their frustration level, and most of all, raise achievement.

LIGHT, DESIGN, AND TIME OF DAY

Three elements that impact over 70 percent of children's learning are light, design, and time of day.[8]

LIGHT
Some students need bright light to concentrate and learn difficult or new information. For others, however, bright light causes headaches, makes it hard to concentrate, and increases hyperactivity. These students read and concentrate best in low light.

DESIGN
Formal design means standard straightbacked school desks in rows. Informal design might be beanbag chairs for reading times or carpet squares to sit on while writing. Some kids learn best in a formal, structured setting, and some in a more informal classroom design.

TIME OF DAY
We all have peak times of the day when we focus, concentrate, and learn the best. The time of day affects the achievement of many students. For example, when offered a choice of courses and times of day, it is better to take the hardest subjects at one's peak time of day. The standardized test score or SAT score will be higher if given at the time of day the student can concentrate and perform best.

Students can't control all the factors at school, but some schools have a rotating class schedule to help with the time-of-day issue, and some teachers provide a part of the classroom with comfortable furniture as an informal reading/writing area. Some teachers who realize bright light is a problem to certain students, install a cover that dims the light slightly or place students who need bright light close to a window.

At home, though, instead of insisting your child sit still at a desk at homework times, you could plan together the design that would work best for your child. You could experiment with bright or low light and see if it makes a difference. If your child needs to filter out noise to concentrate better, he or she could wear a "dead" Walkman headset or listen to light classical music in the background if some sound is needed.

CHAPTER TWELVE

KEEPING YOUR CHILD ON TRACK

A aron, a seventh grader, bolted in the door after his first week of school, threw his backpack on the floor, and handed his crumpled history report to his mother.

"Good grade, Aaron," she said, looking over the report.

"Yeah, no big deal—it's the easy class. I'm in there with all the dumb kids, and I miss my friends," he replied.

Thousands of kids like Aaron all over North America feel dumb because they're assigned to low- and average-track classes where they are exposed to lower content levels, cover less material during the year, and develop significantly lower self-esteem than their classmates in enriched or high-track courses. Many of these students have learning differences, but need the enrichment and challenge of higher-level classes.

In a personal interview, Jane Healy, Ph.D., author of *Your Child's Growing Mind*, said, "I have known many children who because of their mechanics of written language, spelling problems, or different way of processing information, were condemned as lazy or not too bright. And although they had fabulous ideas and extremely good comprehension—they are often excluded from top-level classes and gifted programs." On the other hand, she added, a lot of good technicians (good in the clerical work of school) end up in the faster tracks but lack the creativity we think "gifted" kids should have.

I think all children have gifts and talents and are thus "gifted," but it is up to parents and teachers to look for and develop these gifts and strengths. (See chapters 9 and 10 for "Another Look at Smart.")

In Aaron's case, when he entered the regional junior high school, he was assigned to Track II (average) classes because of his standardized test scores and poor handwriting. The teacher felt he would experience less frustration and make higher grades in the slower-paced classes. But not only did he feel isolated from his best friends, with whom he'd gone through elementary school, but his motivation and confidence also slid because there was little challenge and his classmates put out little effort. Aaron was one of those students who rose to whatever was expected of him. In fact, research shows that even talented, high-ability kids get B's and C's when put in low-level classes.[1]

As the semester went on, his parents began to realize that little homework was assigned and that the quality of instruction was not as high, nor the climate as serious, as in the higher track. Aaron's mother talked with the teacher about her concerns, but no changes were made. Not wanting to rock the boat and cause trouble for him, she thought, *We'll get through this year and surely the school will discover he needed to be in Track I classes.*

However, the next year Aaron was again assigned to average classes for eighth grade. So his parents took action. They met with the guidance counselor and shared Aaron's previous record, an outside evaluation that showed his IQ was in the above-average range, and their belief that he could rise to the teachers' expectations in the higher classes. They also expressed their willingness to get him tutoring or any support needed.

Due to their intervention, Aaron was changed to Track I classes for three of his subjects. And with extra help with organization and study skills from home, some tutoring in math by a college-aged study buddy, and a lot of encouragement, he made the honor roll by the end of the year. He also grew in the confidence that he could stand on his own in the most rigorous classes the school had to offer. Then for ninth grade he was assigned to all top-level classes.

TRACKING, AND HOW IT AFFECTS YOUR CHILD

Aaron's situation reflects one of the hottest issues in education today: tracking. Having different levels of subjects for students of similar ability—either within the class or in a separate room—is a much-debated topic in education circles, and it is critical that parents be informed, involved advocates for their children. Although in many states and school districts, efforts are being made to do away with low tracks altogether and beef up the academic programs for all kids—and there is much discussion about the practice—tracking or ability grouping persists in most schools in the United States. While some schools are going to heterogeneous groupings (mixed-ability classes for academic subjects), approximately 60 percent of elementary schools and 80 percent of secondary schools still have tracking or ability grouping.[2] More public schools than private schools have tracking, but you can also find grouping in private schools.

It may be great if your child is in the enriched, gifted, top-track classes. In fact, I feel that, at least in public schools, unless your child is in the honors or high-track classes in high school, he or she is probably getting a very mediocre education.

But what if your child is assigned to average or low-track classes? Much less effort is required, academic standards are lower, and because high-level classes cover more complex material at a faster pace than low groups, the gap between high and low achievers widens more every year. That means your child gets farther behind every year. The second grader in the "Buzzard," or low, reading group becomes the high schooler in the basic/remedial English course who likely will not get the writing skills necessary for college success. That's why it is important to intervene as early as possible in your child's schooling to make sure he or she doesn't "fall through the tracks." If your child is in the low reading group in first or second grade, that should be a red flag that he or she needs extra support.

In the early grades, parents need to make sure kids are mastering the basic skills in the three R's so they will be equipped with the thinking and language skills necessary to handle challenging work in later grades. It's critical that you stay on top of your child's education, deal with problems quickly, and stay involved with the school.

Reading is the most important academic skill (although math is vital, too) because almost 90 percent of all school subjects require reading. If your child's reading skills aren't up to par, get him or her extra tutoring outside of school, using a method that builds on the child's learning-style strengths, and read aloud a lot at home—but don't accept a "reading disabled" label. (See ways to help children of different strengths or weaknesses to learn to read and promote fluency and comprehension in chapter 8, "How Learning Styles Impact Reading Skills.")

ADVOCATING FOR YOUR CHILD

Here's what you can do as an advocate for your child in a school with tracking or ability grouping:

Gather all the information you can. Many parents I have talked to have no idea which ability group or level of courses their child is in. Yet in one large middle school or junior high, there can be five or more levels of language and math classes. Talk to teachers, guidance counselors, and other parents at the beginning of the year to find out about ability grouping at your child's school. Schools may not offer or advertise this information, but you need it to act as an advocate for your child. Ask questions like the following:

- In which subjects and grade levels are students grouped—in math and language arts only, or in all classes? Sometimes if students are grouped in several classes, scheduling necessitates putting them in the same group for the rest of the classes. Flexibility in scheduling is best, such as assigning a child talented in math to the high math group but to an average English group (if extra work is needed in the basics). Frequent reevaluation is also necessary so the child can move up and not get stuck.

- What kind of textbooks, activities, and materials are used in each level of the course?
- What are class-level assignments based on? Often standardized test scores, behavior, and prior school achievement are the bases for decisions. But sometimes (especially in elementary school) handwriting, social skills, oral language ability, or subjective factors are strong considerations. Your child may be delayed in one area but quite bright in all the others.

Don't accept a low class placement just because of standardized test scores. The possibility for error is large, and there are many aspects of intelligence pencil-and-paper testing cannot evaluate. As one educator said, "They are making big decisions about little kids (especially in the early grades) when they don't know what a child is really capable of, and the decisions have very important consequences." Being put in the low-achieving group can become a self-fulfilling prophecy—made on minor criteria, it becomes major and reinforces itself. Remember, children will live up or down to our expectations.

Some children are not good test takers but have above-average or even superior intelligence. In fact, although the criterion for high-level classes may be scoring in the ninetieth percentile, students from the fiftieth percentile on up are capable of doing work in the higher track and are too often assigned to the lower track.[3] While we can consider the evaluations the school provides, we can also trust our own sense about our children and their ability.

Talk to your child about what his or her goals are and what your hopes are. Then make sure the school courses line up with the requirements in the field of study, including college work, postgraduate work, and technical training. The middle school grades are not too early to start planning, because courses taken then, like pre-algebra, set the stage for beginning algebra in ninth grade, and then the higher-math courses needed for college. Without these "gate-keeping courses," or prerequisites, your child may miss out on other opportunities.

If there are various levels of courses, try to have your child assigned to the highest-level class that he or she can be successful in. Sarah's standardized test scores started out in the fiftieth percentile in the early grades, but her mother always requested the most challenging classes. Sometimes she needed help with studying or a written report. Her mother also had her on a stimulating reading program at home in which she was continually, throughout elementary and middle school, reading the classics both aloud with her family and silently on her own. Now in the eighth grade, her test scores are in the eightieth and ninetieth percentiles, and she qualified for honors English and other top-level classes.

You may face some resistance from the school, such as, "I don't think your child can handle the more difficult material." You could respond, "Let her have a temporary placement of three to five months in the higher track to see how she does. We will provide support at home. If it means extra work, we will help her or get her a tutor." Then the school knows that the assistance will be there for the student to be successful.

You do need to be realistic about your child's age and developmental level when you evaluate whether your child is ready for advanced math. Also, be sure to consider the prior math teacher's recommendation of abstract thinking ability. When Katie was at the end of sixth grade, her parents learned that seventh-grade students would be separated into algebra and basic math review groups. The algebra course was to be taught in an abstract way rather than in a hands-on way, and some seventh graders are not ready for it.

Her parents decided Katie needed to be in advanced math, since she was so bright in language subjects and in the other top classes. However, she was good but not excellent in math. She floundered by the middle of the year and had to be put in the lower math. "There's a fine line; but in math, especially if there's any doubt, don't push students ahead," says Jane Healy, a specialist in children's brain development. "One research study showed even gifted math students who were accelerated too soon ended up believing they were not smart in math."[4] At the same time, a child who can do all the math and comprehend it easily will become bored if not accelerated to his or her ability level.

If your child does move to a higher-level class or group, inform him or her that the new class is going to be challenging, and that there may even be some catching up to do, but support will be provided. In order to make a good transition, the parents, teacher, *and* child need to be willing to put out extra effort. The student and teacher might agree to one-on-one instruction two days a week during the regular study/extra-help period for a while. Or the parents may agree to spend thirty minutes each night helping, or to find a tutor. The student might need help getting better organized or be equipped with strategies in his or her strongest modality from this book to use for study. The student might need to use a lap-top computer in class or tape lectures and chapters for review, or implement one of the modifications listed in chapter 11.

Do let the school know you'll be checking back in a few weeks to see how your child is doing with the new assignment! Participate in school-improvement committees to encourage the school to provide a top-notch academic program for *all* the students—to improve teaching and have smaller classes; and to get parents involved in enrichment, assisting in classrooms, and supporting education at home. And most of all, let your child know you believe in him or her 100 percent, and instead of pressure, give a lot of encouragement, which we will discuss in the next chapter.

CHAPTER THIRTEEN

ENCOURAGING AND MOTIVATING YOUR CHILD

"What's the difference between encouragement and pressure?" This is a question moms and dads often ask in seminars I present to PTAs and parents' meetings at schools. They don't want to burn their child out or discourage him or her with pressure from school and home, but often they are frustrated that the grades aren't higher.

What do you do when you're disappointed with your child's performance, or think your child can do better? What do you say when you are trying to "light a fire" under him or her? We all get exasperated, and sometimes say things like: "You could do better," "Why don't you study more, like your sister who gets straight A's?" and "If you don't pass this semester, they'll have to hold you back" (a very threatening thought to every kid!).

I've even heard parents—when pushed to their frustration limit— say: "If you don't straighten up and bring up your grades, you're going to military school" and "At the rate you're going, you'll never get an education or be successful!"

Explains Dr. Carol Kelly, a school psychologist, "As much as we know the negative approach doesn't work, it's amazing how often parents resort to it when upset with their children's performance." Even without our negative comments, many children fear they won't get a job after graduation. All they have to do is look at the economic forecasts on the nightly news to be worried.

"I worry about how successful I'll be and what I'm going to do when I grow up," said an eighth-grade girl. "Now my parents buy everything, but I wonder if I'm going to be able to take care of kids or if I'll become a bag lady and live in a slum." Anxiety, however, is a poor motivator. In fact, the child filled with anxiety has a hard time concentrating in the classroom.

EMOTIONAL NURTURING

According to Dr. Jane Healy, emotional nurturing is the most important job of parents. The sense of safety, nurturing, and emotional security—which includes parentally imposed behavioral limits in the early years and meeting children's needs—is what comprises children's motivation systems. If we do not build a sense of emotional security in our child, "we'll end up with a child with a serious motivation problem, one who *could* learn and achieve but *won't*." In fact, says Dr. Healy, the brain does not develop to its capacity and the child does not mentally grow to his or her potential without that sense of emotional security.[1]

No school, no matter how excellent the curriculum or teachers, can provide what parents can—namely, a trusting, stable relationship with their child. That relationship forms the core of the child's self-worth and influences the child's decisions, choice of friends, and ability to learn. And the stable home base is an anchor that gives him or her the peace of mind and inner security to concentrate on reading, writing, and other studies.

Thus, what looks on the surface like a learning disability can be evidence of anxiety and turmoil in the child, which can block learning by as much as 90 percent.[2] Nathan was a bright, enthusiastic student in kindergarten and the beginning of first grade. Then because his parents were in conflict, the climate at home became unpredictable, distracting, and lacking in emotional security. The end result was divorce, and big transitions for Nathan and his mother as she attempted to provide for him as a single parent. During this time, although he was a bright little boy, Nathan did not learn to read or do basic math. He failed first grade and became a behavior problem at school. And it took two years of private tutoring and the stabilization of their home environment before he was able to achieve at grade level.

Our home environments actually shape children's growing brains as we provide the foundations for them to thrive.[3] Our children may go through difficult times or face challenges at school or in their lives, but their time at home, especially in the early years, will set the stage for their patterns of behavior, relationships, and learning.

A big part of emotional nurturing centers on providing an atmosphere of encouragement in the family. The child who is constantly encouraged has a much greater chance of succeeding in school and life. The child who lives with en*courage*ment (the root word being *courage*) develops courage and confidence. And there are many research studies that show the power of encouragement: that children who are motivated do well in school, and that those who have the inner strength to keep trying despite obstacles have parents who are like quiet cheerleaders who have positive expectations but are not demanding. If their child is unsuccessful in some undertaking, they don't make a big deal out of it. They talk about it; the child is encouraged to learn from it and try again. Positive words, smiles, and physical affection are frequent. They share in their child's excitement and interests. And the most important secret of all—they cheer and appreciate their child's *efforts* as opposed to just his or her ability.

This gets back to our original question—what's the difference between encouragement and pressure? Pressure focuses on the results, the A's on the report card (because nothing else is worthy of applause), winning and being the best in sports and competition. But encouragement focuses on efforts, improvement, and progress.

The word *encouragement* means faith, help, support, confidence, reassurance, incentive, hope, and a shot in the arm! How desperately our children and teens need these. They are more stressed than any generation before them because our society is fast-paced, competitive, and full of pressure. One study showed that over two million schoolchildren take prescribed medication to counteract the effects of stress and tension in their lives.[4] Depression and suicide are the second-leading cause of teenage death. Our children especially need support and encouragement:

- when they have problems (which occurs almost daily).
- when they go through transitions (childhood and especially adolescence is one big transition), moving to a different school, or changes in the family.
- when they are trying hard and not succeeding.
- when they are late bloomers.
- when they have learning differences that cause them difficulties in reading or other subjects in their education.

Encourage is an action verb meaning to support, cherish, inspire, cheer up, stimulate, approve, spur, fortify, brace, strengthen, and root for. How can we encourage children and teens—our own, certainly, but also those in our life, car pools, and neighborhood?

Smiles

Smiles are an important sign of affirmation, approval, warmth, and caring to children. We sometimes use negative techniques like frowning at children and expressing displeasure at what they're doing or failing to do. But children see themselves in the mirrors we hold up to them in our facial expressions—our smiles or frowns, our acceptance or disapproval. Their mental picture of themselves is important—if it's one they can like, they grow in confidence and motivation, for they see themselves reflected in our eyes, smiles, words, and opinions.

Although all children need to see smiles, visual children are very sensitive to the facial expressions of the significant people in their lives, and receive special encouragement through our smiles and looks of approval.

Sometimes as parents and teachers we think what is most important is the content and lessons we are teaching children. I received a letter from a student that showed me otherwise. I had been doing creative-writing workshops with elementary school classes for a few weeks—helping them write poems, publish books, and stories. Here's what Sara wrote:

Dear Mrs. Fuller,
    Thank you so much. You have taught me so many things. I really appreciate you coming. I hope you like our classroom. I love the way that you always walk in our classroom with a smile on your face. Thank you so much.

From Sara Hawkins

Physical Affection

Hugs, pats, and other signs of physical affection meet children's emotional needs and are great forms of encouragement. For the kinesthetic and tactile learners, perhaps the most important way of showing love and caring is through hugs.

All children, but especially our active, physically oriented "doers and touchers," need hugs and kisses. And if they don't get them at home, they often come to school emotionally needy and restless; they act out or agitate others as a way to get the attention they need. Kinesthetic learners tend to communicate by touching, and they respond to physically expressed encouragement, such as a pat on the back.

WHAT'S SO GREAT ABOUT HUGS?

There is no such thing as a bad hug. They are not fattening and they don't cause cancer or cavities. They are all-natural with no preservatives, artificial ingredients, or pesticide residue.

They are cholesterol-free, naturally sweet, 100-percent wholesome, and a completely renewable resource. Hugs don't require batteries, tune-ups, or X-rays. They are nontaxable, fully returnable, and energy-efficient. They are safe in all kinds of weather. In fact, they are especially good for cold and rainy days. And they are exceptionally effective in treating problems like bad dreams and disappointments.

The moral: Never wait until tomorrow to hug someone you could hug today.

Studies show everyone needs at least four hugs, pats, or signs of physical affection a day just to survive; eight for good mental health; and twelve to be really motivated and enthusiastic about life. And kids need hugs the most when they are the *least lovable*—when they've had a hard day at school, have friend problems, or are under stress. Hugs fill up their emotional tank so they have the energy they need to tackle school and other challenges.

Listening

Another way to encourage and emotionally nurture and support our children and teens is through listening.

"For many kids," said a counselor, "the world can seem like a fearsome landscape in which Geraldo's guests appear normal—that's where parents should come in, to help moderate the normal and predictable fears of childhood and adolescence."

LISTEN TO YOUR CHILDREN

Take a moment to listen today
To what your children are trying to say
Listen today, whatever you do
Or they won't be there to listen to you
Listen to their problems
Listen for their needs
Praise their smallest triumphs
Praise their smallest deeds
Tolerate their chatter
Amplify their laughter
Find out what's the matter
Find out what they're after
But tell them that you love them
Every single night
And though you scold them
Make sure you hold them
And tell them—"Everything's all right!
Tomorrow's looking bright!"
Take a moment to listen today
To what your children are trying to say
Listen today, whatever you do
And they will come back to listen to you. *(Anonymous)*

Shared time, talk, and someone to listen are the very best medicine for many of the difficulties young people have.

Of all the modalities, auditory learners have the greatest desire to be listened to. They are the most sensitive to tone of voice, and appreciate a listening ear for all the thoughts and ideas they have to share. Since they actually solve problems and work out difficulties best by talking about them, a great gift to give them is patient, attentive listening.

When we listen, we discover what kids are interested in, what they need, and where they are hurting. Sometimes a parent or teacher who listens and cares is like a life preserver to a child who is struggling. The encouragement of listening helps the child keep going and keep trying.

Appreciation and Invitation

Another way to encourage and emotionally nurture is to appreciate the uniqueness of each young person—a one-of-a-kind child, with a distinct learning style, different gifts and talents—and, as we have discussed in this book, to build on his or her strengths. Nothing builds a child's self-esteem more than this.

"When someone is deprived of his self-esteem, he is deprived of the one thing that makes a person worth loving. For one's own benefit, if for no other reason, the effort should be to build self-esteem in the other, to confirm rather than to assault it. This is achieved, not by flattery, but by a generous appreciation of the other's strengths and a generous deemphasis of weaknesses, by speaking of his good points and as rarely as possible about his bad ones," said Jo Coudert.[5]

Seeing something promising in each child—an attitude, an intelligence gift, a talent for painting or for mechanical things—can make a great difference. One day as I worked with fifth graders in an elementary school near our city, it was time for "Reader's Theatre," which was an opportunity for students to share their poetry and family stories with the whole section of fifth graders. I read through all the pieces to pick several for that day's "Reader's Theatre," and noticed one called "My Hand," by Brandy. It was a lovely poem, and although I didn't know which of the fifty-five students was Brandy (she was not one of the "out front" type of kids you notice), I called her up to the front and gave an introduction of her poem.

A shy girl, sitting all alone at the back of the room, walked to the front. With long blonde hair, her blue eyes looking down, she smiled quietly and began to read her poem. After she had finished, I told her what a wonderful piece of expression it was, and the class audience affirmed it—they liked Brandy's poem, too, and told her. After class she and I talked about how she could send it out to a children's magazine for possible publication. For the next two weeks while I worked each day with the class creating personal-experience stories and limericks, sensory poetry, and an anthology of their best works, Brandy continued to share her writing with me, and I continued to encourage her.

She sent me this letter after my "writer's residency" there was over:

> Dear Mrs. Fuller,
>
> These few weeks have been the best days of my life. You brought out the person that I didn't realize I had. I'll always remember you and cherish you for what you did for me. Here are a few things I wrote: (she included some poems).
> Your enthusiastic student,
>
> Brandy

Just a little encouragement went a long way. William James said the deepest principle in human nature is the craving to be appreciated. We as parents and teachers need to be *finders*, treasure hunters, looking for the spark God has put in each child—the gifts, abilities, and interests. Regardless of their problems, handicaps, or prickly personalities, we can look for and discover the best that is within our children, and not withhold our encouragement and affirmation until they're better or older, less messy, or making all A's—but enjoy and appreciate them right where they are!

Positive Words

Another way to emotionally support young people is with our words, spoken and written. We want our kids to improve—to clean their messy rooms, make higher grades, have better behavior, practice the piano more. We see all their foibles up close and so we do a lot of correcting—especially perfectionistic parents who look for a "perfect ten" performance from their child before offering compliments. A survey found that mothers criticized ten times more than they gave a positive comment to their children. We all have bad days when we're stressed, and it pours out on our family. Sentences like "Grow up!" "You never do what I tell you!" and "Where'd you get a crazy idea like that? No, you can't go!" may be frequent. Instead try substituting phrases like these that provide encouragement, understanding, and support:

- "I love you."
- "I know you can do it."
- "That's okay, nobody's perfect."
- "You really are improving."
- "I'm proud of you."
- "Let's sit down and talk about this."
- "Thanks for your help."
- "I really appreciate your (fill in the blank)!"
- "I'm sorry. Will you forgive me?"
- "What's your opinion?"
- "You are really growing up."

A single positive comment spoken to our child can make a huge difference. Also, a simple written note can offer powerful encouragement. It can brighten the child's day, motivate, and plant seeds that grow for a long time. Often when people receive an encouraging note, it is tucked away in a book or desk and taken out on a hard day when it does its magic, lifting the spirit again.

Lunch-box love notes are great for kids of all ages, and even pre-readers will try to figure out what the message says (rebus-type messages with simple words and pictures substituting for some words help younger children). Written notes are an especially fine way to communicate with adolescents who may be a little "prickly," disinterested in long chats with Mom and Dad, or maybe just busy. So much can be said in a personal note—be it practical information and directions like "Please take out the trash and clean your room before leaving for the movie"; an encouraging word that shows we are tuned in: "I know this has been a hard week, what with your girl-friend breaking up with you and your not making the team. I feel your hurt. If you want to talk, I'm here"; or maybe just a pep-up note: "You put some real studying into the history exam! I know you'll do well!"

When you become a note-writing family, you'll find that your child or teen begins to leave notes for you, like one Alison left taped to the door one day: "Mom and Dad, I have good news!! (Tell ya later.) Ashley and I are looking for a birthday present for Amanda. I'll be back shortly. Hope you both had a great day! I love you, Alison." Or one she left in my room to express appreciation: "Thank you for being such a good mom and nurse while I was sick. Thanks for being caring and helpful to me. I love you very much! I'll be praying for you on your speaking trip. Don't forget to have a little fun too! Love you, Ali." Sometimes they express a little need: "Mom—could you make some tapioca pudding today? Thank you. Love, Ali."

Your note doesn't have to be long—just a few sentences, with a genuine compliment, word of thanks, or praise.

BELIEVING IN YOUR CHILD

No matter how your children are doing right now, no matter what problems or struggles they are experiencing, keep believing in them, have high hopes and realistic expectations they can meet, and they'll grow in confidence and motivation. Their motivation is fueled by our hope and belief in them—that they do have strengths and gifts, and that with hard work and persistence, they will bloom. That although they may be developing slower physically or intellectually, or may learn differently from other students, they have talents and are full of promise.

Jim Trelease tells of his brother Brian, who was always in reme-dial reading classes. Of four boys in their family, he took the longest to graduate from college, but was the only one to graduate with honors and the only one who got a master's degree. He is also the only one of the brothers to become a CEO of a major corporation. He tells how his father, who must have sensed Brian had some spark of business savvy, read the *Wall Street Journal* every night to him, while upstairs Jim thought, *How silly; he doesn't even understand it and couldn't read it himself.* Now Brian runs ads in the *Wall Street Journal.*[6]

Another person who faced huge obstacles, Norma Claypool had both eyes removed at two years old due to a malignant brain tumor. But her four-foot-nine-inch mother wouldn't let her accept any limitations or feel sorry for herself. She constantly encouraged her and drilled into her these words: "You can do anything you want!"

Norma graduated magna cum laude from the University of Pittsburgh in two and a half years. Though blind, she became a certified special-education teacher and consultant. She went on to get her master's degree and doctorate in special education. And she now single-handedly cares for ten handicapped children she adopted.[7] Her mother's belief in her made the difference.

We are tempted to write many kids off academically. But let me encourage you not to write them off—not to let a teacher write them off—not ever to give up on them. Instead, show them how to capitalize on their learning-style strengths and develop their gifts. Keep believing in them and providing the verbal, physical, emotional, and spiritual support they need to succeed. Even with tremendous obstacles, if a child is believed in and encouraged, he or she can accomplish amazing things.

Chapter Fourteen

HELPING STUDENTS FIND THEIR LEARNING STRENGTHS
A Unit for Home Or School

T he following pages contain a short week-long unit of study you can use to help students discover their own learning-style preferences. The activities can be done at home with parents or at school in the classroom. It is also ideal for home-schoolers. When siblings and/or classmates realize each other's strengths, they can find ways to be more supportive, appreciate one another's gifts, and work together.

One of the problems that many children, especially underachievers, have is not knowing how their brains work and what helps them learn. They may study by reading over the notes and text, fail to remember the information, and then be frustrated at the poor results. They may "study" a spelling list and then have only 50-percent recall of the correct words on the test. But when the light bulb goes on about what their strengths are and how they can use them to study smarter, it sparks their motivation and helps them become more active students who take responsibility for their learning. They can usually see a rise in grades, and the encouragement from that builds momentum to try other study strategies that work best for their learning style.

DAY ONE: OVERVIEW OF LEARNING STYLE

Share with your child all about learning style, what "perceptual strength" means, and how auditory, kinesthetic, and visual learners process information; how environmental factors affect our learning, such as sound (do you learn best in a quiet environment or with background music or noise?), light, peak time of day to learn, with a partner or alone, etc. Students can talk about the elements that help them learn new or hard information.

I introduce the topic by saying something like this:

> Your knowledge and understanding about your learning strengths are like *tools* we keep in the car in case of a flat tire or car trouble. It would be nice if your teacher's or parent's way of teaching always matched or complemented yours— but it won't. Everyone is different. Since you want to learn the most you can in all your subjects, you need to have strategies that work with the way you think and learn. Then your own study methods are there when you have new or difficult material to tackle, when you have tests to study for, or when you and your teacher are not on the same beam. You'll also learn flexibility (the ability to respond to change and new situations), a valuable life skill, and be able to succeed more in your academics.

DAY TWO

Take a learning-style survey (see appendix for a listing of surveys). Score it, evaluate it, and discuss what your child discovered about his or her learning style.

DAY THREE

Make posters to represent your child's preferences. The poster can be made in the shape of something that is important to his or her study time. One student made her poster in the shape of a light bulb because she needed good light to concentrate. Another made her poster in the shape of a bed because she liked to study on her bed. One even made hers in the shape of her dog because she liked him to be next to her when she studied at her desk.

Inside the poster have the child write and draw pictures about his or her learning-style preferences, favorite subjects, strengths, and needs. Here is what some children wrote:

- I like to study alone.
- I like quiet.
- I learn best in the morning.
- I like to study with a friend.
- I need a snack when I study.
- I need an organized desk.
- I am an auditory/kinesthetic learner.
- My favorite subject: Science.
- I like long-term projects.
- I like to learn things step by step.
- I have a good visual memory.

Materials needed for this exercise are a white or colored poster board, markers, pencils, scissors, and rulers.

DAY FOUR AND FOLLOWING

Each student makes a learning center on a subject he or she is interested in (examples: raccoons, constellations, heraldry, spiders, aerospace, World War II history, etc.). The learning center needs to present information on the subject and provide learning activities for all modalities.

Brainstorm together on strategies and things to include. For example, the bone display at the Children's Museum of Boston, which we can use as a prototype of sorts, included the following:

- X-rays to look at
- broken bones to pick up
- bones of a sheep to assemble with model above (kinesthetic)

- information and facts written on the wall to read silently (visual) or aloud (auditory)
- bones of different animals to see (visual)
- a computer game (visual, kinesthetic)

One student made his learning center on electronics. It included color pictures on display; activity cards; a word-find activity; a resistor, transistor, and capacitator he made; and an electronic question-and-answer board with these instructions: "Touch one wire to a question terminal, take the other wire, touch it to the correct answer, and the light will light up."

A center on the state of Vermont included a report, a map, an interview with a maple syrup farmer with photos, and task cards. A learning center on constellations included a star guide, a fill-in-the-blanks exercise, task cards with activities, an activity entitled "Connect the Constellation to the Star That Is in It," and a written report.

These learning centers can be started at school and completed at home, and they may take a number of school days to finish.

DAY FIVE

After the learning center is completed, ask the children to share it with someone: their class, a younger class, family members, or a home-schooling group. They may even convince the school librarian to display it for a few days. Encourage any who see the learning center to do the activities on it.

DAY SIX

Hand out a sheet of study strategies entitled "Study Smarter." Explore and discuss the best ways for each student to study based on what he or she has discovered about learning strengths. Have the children make their own list called "Study Smarter, Not Harder." Then try at least one new study strategy on the next chapter of history, science, or other subject they need to learn. Evaluate and discuss the results; then try other strategies.

RESOURCES ON LEARNING STYLES AND RECOMMENDED BOOKS

RESOURCES

Cuisenaire Company of America, Inc.
12 Church Street, Box D
New Rochelle, NY 10802
(800)237-3142

> Catalog with manipulatives and many hands-on materials, including centimeter rods and Cuisenaire rods, to teach math and science. Can be used at home or school.

"Guidelines for Young Writers: How to Get Published"
P.O. Box 770493
Oklahoma City, OK 73120

> For guidelines on how and where to send your young writer's work for possible publication, send a self-addressed, stamped envelope to the above address. Also refer to Market Guide for Young Writers in recommended book list.

Hawthorne Educational Service, Inc.
800 Gray Oak Drive
Columbia, MO 65201
(800)542-1673
(314)874-1710

A valuable resource for dealing with the most common learning and behavior problems encountered in a learning environment is PRIM, the Pre-Referral Intervention Manual. Catalog of resources available.

Keeping Track: Student Assignment Planner
Teaching Children to Teach Themselves
Success in School
Karen DeClouet
415 Kyle Landry
New Iberia, LA 40560

Learning Styles Network
8000 Utopia Park
Jamaica, NY 11439
(718)990-6335

Hands-on materials, books, and other resources available for teachers or parents on learning styles; inventory and surveys available to evaluate learning style.

Math Alive!
Educational Strategies for Mathematical Competency
Elaine D. Gaines
P.O. Box 74
Hot Sulphur Springs, CO 80451

Curriculum consultation and resources.

Mind's Eye
P.O. Box 1060
Petaluma, CA 94953
(800)227-2020

Catalog that includes many books on tape for students of all
ages. A wide selection of children's classics, music tapes. Great
American series, including Thomas Edison, Benjamin
Franklin, Ann Morrow Lindbergh, and more. Excellent
resource for home learning.

Orton Dyslexia Society
Chester Building, Suite 382
8600 LaSalle Road
Baltimore, MD 21286-2044
(410)296-0232

Write to the above address for information on Alphabetic
Phonics and other multi-sensory methods of learning to read.

Parents Sharing Books
Family Literacy Center
2805 East 10th Street, Suite 150
Bloomington, IN 47408-2698
(812)855-5847

For more information on this program write to the above
address.

Price Systems, Inc.
P.O. Box 1818
Lawrence, KS 66044
(913)843-7892

Learning-style inventory for various grades; computerized
printout of results, and manual.

Recorded Books
6306 Aaron Lane
Clinton, MD 20435
(800)638-1304

Catalog includes excellent selection of children's classic books and stories on tape, music, and activity tapes.

Science-by-Mail
Museum of Science
Science Park
Boston, MA 02114
(800)729-3300

Hands-on problem-solving science kits for children from fourth to ninth grade. Scientists evaluate children's experiments and correspond by mail.

Spalding Education Foundation
5930 West Greenway, Suite 4
Glendale, AZ 85306
(602)547-2656

Contact this foundation for more information on total language arts method, including phonics, grammar, reading, and writing.

Storytelling Circle
Weston Woods
Weston, CT 06883

Catalog with fine storytelling tapes.

Touch Math
Innovative Learning Concepts
6760 Corporate Drive
Colorado Springs, CO 80919-1999
(800)888-9191

A multi-sensory approach to basic computation and other beginning math subjects. It is designed for students K-3 and used remedially through adult education classes.

Visual Phonics
International Communication Learning Institute
7108 Bristol Boulevard
Edina, MN 55435
(612)929-9381

Information on Alphabetic Phonics and other multi-sensory methods of learning to read is available from the above address.

RECOMMENDED BOOKS

Armstrong, Thomas. *In Their Own Way.* Los Angeles: Tarcher, 1987.

Bradway, Lauren, and Barbara Hill. *How to Maximize Your Child's Learning Ability.* Garden City, NY: Avery Publishing, 1993.

Burron, Arnold. *Helping Kids Cope: A Parents' Guide to Stress Management.* Elgin, IL: Accent, 1988.

Campbell, Ross. *How to Really Love Your Child.* Wheaton, IL: Victor, 1986.

Campbell, Ross. *How to Really Love Your Teenager.* Wheaton, IL: Victor, 1986.

Dunn, Rita. *Teaching Elementary Students Through Their Individual Learning Styles.* Boston: Allyn and Bacon, 1993.

Dunn, Rita. *Teaching Secondary Students Through Their Individual Learning Styles.* Boston: Allyn and Bacon, 1993.

Fuller, Cheri. *Helping Your Child Succeed in Public School.* Colorado Springs, CO: Focus on the Family, 1993.

Fuller, Cheri. *HOME-LIFE: The Key to Your Child's Success at School.* Tulsa, OK: Honor Books, 1988.

Fuller, Cheri. *How to Grow a Young Music Lover.* Wheaton, IL: Harold Shaw, 1994.

Fuller, Cheri. *Motivating Your Kids from Crayons to Career: How to Boost Your Child's Learning and Achievement Without Pressure.* Tulsa, OK: Honor Books, 1990.

Gardner, Howard. *Frames of Mind: The Theory of Multiple Intelligences.* New York: Basic Books, 1983.

Gardner, Howard. *Multiple Intelligences: The Theory in Practice.* New York: Basic Books, 1993.

Golick, Margie. *Deal Me In! The Use of Playing Cards in Teaching and Learning.* New York: Monarch Press, 1981.

Healy, Jane. *Is Your Bed Still There When You Close the Door? How to Have Intelligent and Creative Conversations with Your Kids.* New York: Doubleday, 1992.

Healy, Jane. *Your Child's Growing Mind.* New York: Doubleday, 1987.

Henderson, H. Jane. *Counseling with Computers: Technology and Techniques.* Lancaster, TX: A 351 Company Book, 1984 (P.O. Box 1174).

Henderson, Kathy. *Market Guide for Young Writers.* Cincinnati, OH: Writer's Digest Books, 1993.

Levine, Mel. *Keeping a Head in School: A Student's Book About Learning Abilities and Learning Disorders.* Toronto: Educators Publishing Service, 1990.

Shapiro, Steven R. *The Learning Connection: Effective Answers to Reading and Learning Difficulties.* Tulsa, OK: Vision Development Center, 1991.

Vail, Priscilla. *Learning Styles: Food for Thought and 130 Practical Tips for Teachers, K-4.* Rosemont, NJ: Modern Learning Press, 1992.

Vail, Priscilla L. *Smart Kids with School Problems: Things to Know and Ways to Help.* New York: Dutton, 1987.

Walker, Barbara J. *Diagnostic Teaching of Reading: Techniques for Instruction and Assessment.* Columbus, OH: Merrill, 1992.

Williams, Linda Verlee. *Teaching for the Two-Sided Mind: A Guide to Right Brain/Left Brain Education.* New York: Simon & Schuster, 1983.

NOTES

Chapter One—No Two Children Learn Alike

1. "Growing Up Dumb," *The Boston Phoenix* (May 29, 1992), section 2.
2. Carol Marshall and Kaye Johns, *Success Strategies for At-Risk Students: Center for Success in Learning Manual* (Dallas: Center for Success in Learning, 1992), page 2:16.
3. C. Mist Harmon, "Experts Say At-Risk Students Need Changes in Teaching," *Tulsa World* (March 9, 1990).
4. Marshall and Johns, page 3:1.
5. Vail, page i.
6. Marshall and Johns, page 3:8.
7. Linda Verlee Williams, *Teaching for the Two-Sided Mind: A Guide to Right Brain/Left Brain Education* (New York: Simon & Schuster, 1983), page 145.
8. *CSL News*, volume 6, number 1 (October–November 1991).

9. Lauren Bradway and Barbara Hill, *How to Maximize Your Child's Learning Ability* (Garden City, NY: Avery Publishing, 1993), pages 238-239.

10. Bradway and Hill, page 239.

11. From an interview with Dr. Don Blackerby, Success Skills Institute, Oklahoma City, Oklahoma.

12. Priscilla Vail, *Smart Kids with School Problems* (New York: Dutton, 1987), page 8.

Chapter Two—Learning-Different People Who Achieved

1. From an interview with John Sabolich.

2. Victor Goertzel and Mildred G. Goertzel, *Cradles of Eminence: A Provocative Study of the Childhoods of over 400 Famous Twentieth-Century Men and Women* (Boston: Little, Brown, 1962), page 265.

3. Goertzel and Goertzel, page 248.

4. Goertzel and Goertzel, page 5.

5. Fred J. Epstein with Elaine Shimberg, "I Don't Accept Children Dying," *Reader's Digest* (February 1993), page 201.

6. Epstein, page 202.

7. Bodie and Brock Thoene, *Writer to Writer* (Minneapolis: Bethany, 1990), pages 39-41.

8. Bud Greenspan, "The Highs and Lows of Greg Louganis," *Parade Magazine* (September 11, 1988), pages 4-6.

9. Greenspan, page 5.

10. Thomas Armstrong, *In Their Own Way* (Los Angeles: Tarcher, 1987), page 141.

11. Glenn Plaskin, *Turning Point: Pivotal Moments in the Lives of America's Celebrities* (New York: Carol Publishing Group, 1992), page 178.

12. Donald Clifton and Paula Nelson, "Win with Your Strengths," *Reader's Digest* (May 1993), pages 76-77.

Chapter Three—Identifying Your Child's Learning Style

1. Susan Lapinski, "Learning Disabilities: Mastering the Challenge," *Child Magazine* (December/January 1992), page 74.

Chapter Four—Discovering Your Own Learning Style

1. Carol Marshall and Kaye Johns, *Success Strategies for At-Risk Students: Center for Success in Learning Manual* (Dallas: Center for Success in Learning, 1992), page 3:4.

Chapter Five—Talkers and Listeners: Auditory Learning

1. Karen DeClouet, *Teaching Children to Teach Themselves* (New Iberia, LA: Success in School, 1992).
2. Rita Dunn, as quoted in Carol Marshall and Kaye Johns, *Success Strategies for At-Risk Students: Center for Success in Learning Manual* (Dallas: Center for Success in Learning, 1992), page 3:10.
3. Linda Verlee Williams, *Teaching for the Two-Sided Mind: A Guide to Right Brain/Left Brain Education* (New York: Simon & Schuster, 1983), page 163.
4. Wanda Draper, *High Expectations* (Oklahoma City, OK: Omni Family Productions, 1993 revised), page 2.
5. Draper, page 2.
6. Williams, page 31.
7. Carol McGehe, "Mathematics the Write Way," *Instructor Magazine* (April 1991), pages 36-38.
8. Draper, page 1.

Chapter Six—Doers and Touchers: Kinesthetic Learning

1. Elaine Gaines, *Math Alive* (Hot Sulphur Springs, CO: Educational Strategies for Mathematical Competency, 1993), pages 5-6.
2. Priscilla Vail, *Learning Styles: Food for Thought and 130 Practical Tips for Teachers, K-4* (Rosemont, NJ: Modern Learning Press, 1992), page 13.
3. Gaines, page 6.
4. Benjamin Spock, "The Best Way to Teach," *Parenting Magazine* (September 1993), pages 113-116.
5. Science-by-Mail kits for fourth to ninth graders are available from the Museum of Science, Science Park, Boston, MA 02114. Telephone (800)729-3300.

6. Ellen Hawkes, "I Had to Grow Up Fast," *Parade Magazine* (January 8, 1989), pages 10-12.

7. Carol Marshall and Kaye Johns, *Success Strategies for At-Risk Students: Center for Success in Learning Manual* (Dallas: Center for Success in Learning, 1992), page 3:26.

8. From an interview with Jerry Bell, middle school teacher in Bryan, Texas.

9. Margie Golick, *Deal Me In! The Use of Playing Cards in Teaching and Learning* (New York: Monarch Press, 1981), pages 9, 117.

Chapter Seven—Watchers: Visual Learning

1. Karen DeClouet, *Teaching Children to Teach Themselves* (New Iberia, LA: Success in School, 1992), page 29.

2. DeClouet, page 29.

3. My thanks to Karen DeClouet for her collaboration on the Recall Note-Taking System and helpful insights on learning styles.

4. DeClouet, page 29.

5. Steven Shapiro, *The Learning Connection* (Tulsa, OK: Vision Development Center, 1991), page 114.

6. Golick, *Deal Me In! The Use of Playing Cards in Teaching and Learning* (New York: Monarch Press, 1981) pages 20-22.

7. Marshall and Johns, page 3:26.

Chapter Eight—How Learning Styles Impact Reading Skills

1. As Dr. Seuss said, "I think killing phonics was one of the greatest causes of illiteracy in this country." The United States has dropped to forty-ninth in world literacy. Approximately 61 percent of seventeen-year-olds can't read high school level material. An excellent resource on reading methods is Rudolf Flesch, *Why Johnny Still Can't Read: A New Look at the Scandal of Our Schools* (New York: Harper & Row, 1981).

2. Rita Dunn, "A Research-based Plan for Students Doing Homework," *Early Years*, vol. 15 (December 1984), pages 45-54.

3. *Center for Success in Learning News* (October–November 1991), vol. 6, no. 1.

4. Analysis of reading methods is adapted from consultations with reading specialists Karen Gale, Tim Campbell, Karen DeClouet; and the resources *Diagnostic Teaching of Reading: Techniques for Instruction and Assessment*, second ed. (Columbus, OH: Merrill, 1992) and Carol Marshall and Kaye Johns, *Success Strategies for At-Risk Students: Center for Success in Learning Manual* (Dallas: Center for Success in Learning, 1992).
5. Many educators feel systematic phonics instruction needs to be added to a whole language program in the early grades to equip students to decode words.
6. Flesch, page 123.

Chapter Nine—Another Look at Smart: Part 1
1. Robert Sternberg, "Second Game: The School's Eye View of Intelligence," in *Language, Literacy, and Culture: Issues of Society and Schooling*, ed. J. A. Langer (Norwood, NJ: Ablex, 1987), pages 25-29; see pages 23-78.
2. Sternberg, page 25.
3. Sternberg, page 25.
4. Robert J. Trotter, "Three Heads Are Better than One," *Psychology Today* (August 1986), pages 56-62.
5. Mel Levine, *Keeping a Head in School: A Student's Book About Learning Abilities and Learning Disorders* (Toronto: Educators Publishing Service, 1990), page 283.
6. Sternberg, as quoted in Trotter, page 59.
7. Sternberg, as quoted in Trotter, page 59.
8. Sternberg, page 25.
9. Sternberg, pages 27-28.
10. Donald Clifton and Paula Nelson, *Soar with Your Strengths* (New York: Delacorte Press, 1992), page 72.
11. Clifton and Nelson, page 60.

Chapter Ten—Another Look at Smart: Part 2
1. Victor Goertzel and Mildred George Goertzel, *Cradles of Eminence: A Provocative Study of the Childhoods of over 400*

Famous Twentieth-Century Men and Women (Boston: Little, Brown, 1962), page xii.

2. Howard Gardner, *Multiple Intelligences: The Theory in Practice* (New York: Basic Books, 1993), page 17.

3. Gardner, *Multiple Intelligences*, page 27.

4. Howard Gardner, *Frames of Mind: The Theory of Multiple Intelligences* (New York: Basic Books, 1983), page 181.

5. Gardner, *Frames of Mind*, pages 385-386.

6. Gardner, *Frames of Mind*, page 162.

7. Glenn Plaskin, *Turning Point: Pivotal Moments in the Lives of America's Celebrities* (New York: Carol Publishing Group, 1992), page 178.

8. Donald Clifton and Paula Nelson, *Soar with Your Strengths* (New York: Delacorte Press, 1992), pages 143-147.

Chapter Eleven—Your Child in the Classroom

1. Carol Marshall and Kaye Johns, *Success Strategies for At-Risk Students: Center for Success in Learning Manual* (Dallas: Center for Success in Learning, 1992), page 2:20.

2. Robert Sternberg, "The Practical Intelligence of Improving Teaching," *The National Teaching and Learning FORUM*, vol. 2 no. 2 (1993), pages 1-2.

3. Priscilla Vail, *Learning Styles: Food for Thought and 130 Practical Tips for Teachers, K-4* (Rosemont, NJ: Modern Learning Press, 1992), page 18.

4. Donald Clifton and Paula Nelson, *Soar with Your Strengths* (New York: Delacorte Press, 1992), page 72.

5. Mel Levine, *Keeping a Head in School: A Student's Book About Learning Abilities and Learning Disorders* (Toronto: Educators Publishing Service, 1990), page 270.

6. Marlene LeFever, "How Our Children Learn," *Today's Better Life* (Winter 1992), page 45.

7. J. Samara, *MEGAT* (1990), app. C.

8. Marshall and Johns, page 3:16.

Chapter Twelve—Keeping Your Child on Track

1. According to research by the Stanford Center for the Study of Families, Children and Youth, Sanford M. Dornbusch, director.

2. "Schools' Tracks and Democracy: Sorting Students by Performance: Efficiency or Elitism?" *New York Times* (April 2, 1993), page 2.

3. Sanford Dornbusch, from an interview.

4. Jane Healy, author of *Your Child's Growing Mind* (New York: Doubleday, 1987), from an interview.

Chapter Thirteen—Encouraging and Motivating Your Child

1. Jane Healy, from an interview. See her excellent books *Your Child's Growing Mind* (New York: Doubleday, 1987) and *Is Your Bed Still There When You Close the Door?* (New York: Doubleday, 1992).

2. From an interview with Dale Jordan, University of Arkansas professor and specialist in learning disabilities.

3. Healy, interview.

4. Darrel Lang and Bill Stinson, *Lazy Dogs and Snoozing Frogs* (La Crosse, WI: Coulee Press, 1988), page 5.

5. Jo Coudert, as quoted in John M. Drescher, *Seven Things Children Need* (Scottdale, PA: Herald Press, 1976), page 18.

6. Jim Trelease, "Turning On the Turned Off Reader," audiotape (Springfield, MA: Reading Tree Productions).

7. Christopher Phillips, "Every Child Has a Right to Love," *Parade Magazine* (December 25, 1988), pages 4-6.

AUTHOR

Cheri Fuller is an experienced educator and has taught every level from elementary to college and is currently an adjunct university professor. She is the author of several previous books and numerous articles in *Family Circle*, CHILD, *Parents of Teenagers*, *Focus on the Family*, and others. She has also appeared on numerous television and radio programs, and is a popular speaker to conferences, parent groups, and teacher seminars. She and her husband, Holmes, live in Oklahoma City with their three children.

Cheri's previous books are: *A Mother's Book of Wit and Wisdom, 365 Ways to Build Your Child's Self Esteem, 365 Ways to Develop Your Child's Values, 365 Ways to Help Your Child Learn and Achieve, How to Grow a Young Music Lover, Helping Your Child Succeed in Public School, Motivating Your Kids From Crayons to Career,* and *Home-Life: The Key to Your Child's Success at School.*

To contact Cheri Fuller, write to:

Cheri Fuller
P.O. Box 770493
Oklahoma City, OK 73177